Dear Prudence

The Story Behind the Song

Prudence Farrow Bruns

ISBN: 1503029883
ISBN 13: 9781503029880
Library of Congress Control Number: 2014919631
CreateSpace Independent Publishing Platform
North Charleston, South Carolina

Cover drawing by Albert Bruns

Dedication

I dedicate this book to my two parents,
John Farrow and Maureen O'Sullivan.

Table of Contents

Prologue

My book's title, *Dear Prudence*, refers to a Beatles song written about me in 1968 in India and recorded for *The White Album*. My main objective in writing this book is to tell the real story behind the song. Why did I want to stay in my room in Rishikesh meditating alone for three months?

For many years, I preferred to stay out of the limelight and let others speculate as to why John Lennon wrote that song. Several years ago, my grandson invited me to his high school to meet his friends. My initial reaction was to ask him why his friends would want to meet his grandmother. He told me to just come. When I arrived, I was treated like a superstar as a large group gathered around me. To my surprise, all of them knew and listened to the Beatles' music. I later informally visited the middle and lower schools and, again, was met by similar crowds of children who all wanted to hear about the Beatles.

The Beatles' music spoke to many in my generation. It was our voice, a collective voice, one of hope and change. Seeing the strong reactions at the schools showed me that this voice is still resonating and being heard. I suddenly felt a responsibility to help keep that voice alive, and because the Beatles' song is about me, I now feel almost duty-bound.

In the years since my time in India, I had become somewhat disillusioned and jaded as my hope for making a better world faded. Maybe it's because I expected change to happen faster and in a more obvious, complete fashion. But these encounters with kids of today's generation woke me up. As I looked around, I realized what were once revolutionary ideas and dreams are now mainstream, be it yoga, meditation, alternative medicine, environmental awareness, sustainability, eating local and organic food, or concepts such as "you are what you eat," "happiness comes from within," and "change the world by changing yourself." I couldn't help but notice that many people now live more consciously.

My book is not only my story but also that of a generation, my generation, coming of age during the era of the Cold War, in which annihilation of the human species with the development of the hydrogen bomb was a reality for the first time—merely the push of a few buttons away. Realizing that if humanity were to survive itself we would have to become more enlightened, many of us experienced a kind of identity crisis. Rejecting the status quo, we looked for answers in the more introspective Eastern philosophies. This required of each of us an inward journey, and we were pioneers in that vein. That's not to say the ideas we explored were completely foreign in the West, but they reached a critical mass with our generation. By venturing into our own consciousness and expanding our awareness through Eastern thought and practices, we spawned a revolution in thinking that still influences our world to this day.

And now my generation is passing the mantle. Take it further and be the solution. Practice meditation. Deepen your awareness by transcending within and anchoring your mind in serenity. Create a better, peaceful world starting with yourself. Within these pages, I share my small story as contribution toward this stupendous legacy. As John Lennon wrote, "You may say I'm a dreamer, but I'm not the only one...."

When people ask me why the Beatles wrote the song about me, I tell them it was because I wanted to meditate more than anything else. Yes, perhaps I wanted to gain spiritual enlightenment before anyone else, as John Lennon has said, but really it was so much more.

My life would have been different—I would have been a different person—had I not been named Prudence. Because of the meaning behind this name, I felt a sense of responsibility or destiny that I had to live up to, influencing everything I would do in my life. It was my father who insisted on giving me the name. My mother wanted to call me Bridget, citing Prudence as too severe. Many of my parents' Hollywood friends advised them against stigmatizing their child with such a name. George Cukor, legendary film director and good friend of my father, wrote, "Do I sound like that horrid, old carping hag that appears at christenings if I say—respectfully and tentatively—that I'm not quite sure of the 'Prudence'? I hanker for Sara, Bridget, etc." But my father held his ground, determined that the baby girl be named after his aunt back in Australia, and so I came to be known as Prudence. I discovered years later, after my father died, that there was no such aunt in Australia or any other relative named Prudence. I would never really know why this name meant so much to my father.

My husband has speculated that when my father lived in Tahiti as a young man, perhaps one of the native women schooled by missionaries was named Prudence. It is true that he kept a scrapbook, which I was shown many times, full of pictures of him with a beautiful Tahitian woman. But he never spoke of that woman in particular, other than to say how beautiful she was.

Because of the name Prudence and the sense of destiny that comes with it, I always felt I had to live up to the highest expectations. People would notice me and ask if I was prudent. Did I even know what prudence means? Or they would tell me I was anything but prudent, so how did I get the name Prudence? I was in second-grade religion class when I first became aware of my name's significance. The class was told that prudence is a cardinal virtue. I felt so proud. Prudence is the sister of wisdom. Prudence is the knowledge of the most Holy of Holies.

Acknowledgements

First and foremost, I thank my husband, Albert Bruns, who always believes in any venture I undertake. With regard to my memoir, I can honestly say that it may have been shelved for good had he not encouraged me to keep writing when I felt certain no one would want to read it. I thank each of my three children—Logan, Paulie, and Willy—who have always supported everything that I do. I also thank my beloved grandchildren for their loving support, especially the older two, Keely and Shen. I want to thank Maria Roach for some of the pictures used in this book.

Preface

Although I was born in Los Angeles, California, my life, as I know it, really began in Rishikesh, India, in 1968. Arriving in New Delhi, India, in mid-January, I traveled to Rishikesh by car with my sister Mia Farrow and Maharishi Mahesh Yogi. My path would then cross with John Lennon and George Harrison as they joined the meditation course also searching inward for their own personal answers.

My new environment was alien to anything I had ever experienced. Maharishi's academy was perched high on a cliff overlooking the Ganges River at the edge of an enormous wild jungle sanctuary. Surrounded by the exotic sounds of the jungle nightlife and feeling particularly vulnerable, I reflected on my life's journey and how it had brought me to this point. The great roar of the Ganges River could be ever heard gently thundering in the background below. I felt the gravity of hundreds of years of great souls who braved the harsh elements of a rugged life to pursue deep meditation alone in the jungles along the Ganges River as it first issues forth from the base of the Himalayan Mountain Range.

My first night in Rishikesh as I lay shivering in my bed beneath layers of blankets, I felt a mixture of elation and apprehension. I had dreamed of coming here to meditate for almost two years and finally it was happening. Yet there was the realization that I would be cloistered thousands of miles away from home with little to no communication for three months of intensive self-reflection and deep meditation. The latter made me feel uneasy as if I was looking over the edge of an enormous precipice, undertaking an unimaginable plunge into the unknown. I told myself that I had asked for this. Driven by a relentless passion to reach deep inside, I had prayed day and night that no matter what the cost I be brought to India to experience the profound wisdom of its ancient sages. Now I was finally here and the reality was both glorious and very frightening. I knew it would be the culmination of my lifetime.

My life up to this point, however misguided, was ultimately a quest for the truth. What does that mean? I was looking to make sense of my existence. This did not necessarily mean intellectual sense but sense to my soul, my core. I needed to find peace, true peace inside myself. This is the story of "Dear Prudence." My spiritual quest began in the most unlikely of places – in Beverly Hills with Hollywood film parents. Nonetheless, it is the sincere journey of a modern seeker no matter how improbable it may appear. In the end, I find my salvation in Rishikesh but I don't want to get ahead of myself.

one

Beginning Life

My early childhood was a happy time. Certainly there were bad moments, but nonetheless, I was very content. We led a life of routine with little change, ideal for any child. Born in 1948, my first memories start at three years old with fleeting moments of infatuation with things around me, such as the thick white billowy afternoon clouds layered across the California sky or, after a rare downfall of rain in Los Angeles, the seemingly exotic pools of water formed around the base of the manicured trees in our yard. I remember at age three my first real crush, as my mother, actress Maureen O'Sullivan, held me in her arms late one evening trying to persuade me to kiss my godfather, movie director Tay Garnet. He was strikingly handsome, and his fondness for me was beguiling. I recall my strong conflicting emotions as she forced me closer to him. As his face touched mine, awkward and embarrassed, I gracelessly licked his cheek.

By age five my memories become a continuum of thought rather than transitory instants. The movie that is my real life begins in the backseat of our Chevy station wagon. It was a summer evening on a

Friday, and we were on our way to a drive-in restaurant for dinner. My mother, whom we referred to as Mum or Mom (she preferred Mum), was at the wheel, and my sister, now-actress Mia Farrow, sat in the front passenger seat. Mia, three years older, was complaining that I was still able to eat hamburgers on Fridays while she had to eat fish. She made herself feel better by asking our mother how much longer before I, too, had to eat fish on Fridays. Clearly, it gave her great pleasure to hear my mother remind me it would be only eight more months. I was barely listening as my attention shifted to the far more salient point: I had eight months before I reached the "age of reason." For a Catholic, this marks an important milestone, a kind of crossing over from the age of innocence. It meant I would be capable of knowing right from wrong and, therefore, be accountable. In my small mind, all I registered was that at six years old, I could enter hell. As my mother and sister bantered back and forth, I felt rising dread growing in my heart—I had only eight months left.

I'm not sure exactly how I came to know about hell. I suspect I had been well schooled by my older siblings, who would have found my naïveté in these matters unbearable, for they never missed a chance to pass on their fears or tribulations. I was one of seven children, three boys and four girls. My mother, like many good Catholics, had wanted ten children, but she was "only blessed with seven." My father, movie director John Farrow, also felt blessed with just seven but for very different reasons; like most, wealthy or not, he wasn't looking forward to paying all those tuitions.

Each one of us was given a good Catholic name. My oldest brother is Michael Damien. Next, in order, comes Patrick Joseph, Maria De Lourdes (Mia), John Charles (Johnny), Prudence Ann, Stephania Margarita (Steffi), and Theresa Magdalena (Tisa). There's a story behind each name, but perhaps the best is Tisa's. My mother had been warned by her doctor to not have any more children, but she could not imagine stopping at six. She had great difficulty during what was to be her final pregnancy and was confined to bed rest for the last six months. The doctors told her it was unlikely the baby would survive. My mother, ever the devout Catholic, in times of trial performed several novenas, a petition of prayers for nine straight days. She finally struck a deal with Saint Therese, "The Little Flower," promising that if the baby survived and was a girl, she'd name the child "Theresa" after her.

At just around six months into the pregnancy, my mother went into labor and was rushed by ambulance to the hospital. The last she remembered, before losing consciousness, was praying. When she awoke, her hospital room was filled with beautiful-smelling roses, the flower of Saint Therese. My mother believed this was a message from the saint. Her prayers had been answered—she had not lost the baby. When she returned home, she regretted her promise. Saint Therese is known for her extreme purity, which can be interpreted as prudishness. My mother prayed about it, and a solution was soon realized—she would counter the excessive purity by giving the child the second name of "Magdalena" after Mary Magdalene, the promiscuous woman whom Jesus forgave. Thus, my sister was called "Teresa Magdalena," eventually shortened to "Tisa."

Each of my siblings played a prominent role in my life at different stages. In my early childhood, Johnny was my best play buddy. I often hung out with him and his friends, and we rode our bicycles all over Beverly Hills. We had a pact that every birthday we would invite each other to the party. My mother allowed us to invite one sibling to our birthday parties, which were often large and full of school friends. Steffi was the most sought-after of all our siblings because she was very good-natured, always laughing. I used to be allowed to take her to school with me and to special events. Later, when we moved to Spain, Mia and I fought bitterly over who got to have Steffi as her roommate and buddy.

Tisa is three years younger than I am. She was a very bright child, and I had fun playing different card games with her whenever I was sick and home from school. Mia and I were separated by three years with one brother, Johnny, between us. Our age difference kept us somewhat apart in our earliest years. We became much closer when we attended Catholic boarding school together. Since then, she and I have shared a lifelong spiritual bond. Patrick and Michael were too old to be within my reach as play pals, but I admired each. Patrick was the artist and very sensitive; I respected his wisdom. Michael represented justice in our family, providing great leadership when he was at the helm.

Neither of our parents was born or raised in America. My mother was from Ireland, my father from Australia. Both were the only members of their families to leave their homelands and plant roots in far-off America. They, like so many immigrants, moved to the United States and diligently pursued their dreams. My father worked as a successful writer and movie director, notably the first Australian movie director in Hollywood. My mother, best known for her recurring role as Jane in the popular *Tarzan* film series of the 1930s and '40s, was employed as an actress intermittently throughout our childhood.

Her real-life role as mother was more as an overseer than an everyday hands-on parent. As a result, we children experienced a parade of various characters whose influences lasted for years to come. Even so, my early life and memories remain joyous. It was a secure period for the family as a whole. We lived in a comfortable ranch-style home in a lovely, sprawling neighborhood along North Beverly Drive. It was a life with seemingly little change.

At this point in my childhood, we never traveled far from home, rarely off the beaten path along Sunset Boulevard to our Malibu beach house and back. I was enthralled by the almost exotic lure that venturing to a nearby community held for me. The Christmas I was seven, a trip into the heart of Los Angeles to see Santa Claus was planned. I was beside myself with excitement, for I had never been into what I thought of as the big city. It also meant we would ride a streetcar. Glued to its window, I looked out excitedly as we began our journey. When we finally entered the outskirts of the city with its many tall buildings, I noticed the greenery of the trees and lawns and the blue sky gradually being replaced by ever-expanding gray cement. I wasn't quite sure why, but I felt unsettled by the growing lack of color. As I watched from the window, my vision was filled with run-down housing and dilapidated buildings with children like me playing in the streets. Fascinated but strangely disturbed, I felt a lingering sense of uncertainty.

When we arrived downtown and saw towering clean glistening buildings and Christmas lights, my excitement returned. People were everywhere, filling the sidewalks and overflowing into the streets. I was disturbed at seeing them crossing the streets (jaywalking) even where there were no streetlights. We were to see Santa Claus in a department store, but I have no memory of meeting Santa—only endless crowds, tall buildings, honking horns, large smoke-spewing buses, and jammed cars. The confusion and noise were like nothing I'd ever seen before, especially in contrast to our pristine quiet orderly neighborhood. But it was the sight of those gray run-down buildings on the way to the city that haunted me and recurred in my mind for many years to come, planting seeds of unrest in my otherwise idyllic world.

During the '50s, we had a stream of temporary helpers. Because my parents worked, the house was divided into separate living quarters—adults and children, each autonomous. The children's quarters had a small kitchen, big playroom, and several bedrooms, while the parents' section had two bedrooms, a kitchen, dining room, den where movies were viewed, and living room. The older boys had rooms off the den. We had a series of live-in governesses and a cook who did most of the cooking and shopping for everyone.

As a result of this division, we lived quite separate lives from our parents. Seeing them somewhat infrequently created an aura of awe and mystery. I saw my father mostly under very cordial circumstances. I suppose I saw him in less formal situations, too, but I remember the pomp that surrounded him back then. It was always a special occasion to see him. Every Sunday afternoon, he had his "regulars," consisting largely of his favorite friends in the local Jesuit population, over for drinks and discussions. They loved to drink and debate literature, religion, and history. We were allowed to sit in if we remained quiet. We children loved those salons and looked forward to them all week. Even though we rarely understood what they were talking about, we listened with fervor as the conversational tones shifted in frequency and volume. When they laughed, we laughed as loud and hard as any of them. When the pitch dropped, becoming more serious, we leaned in to listen intently, just like the others.

Sometimes my father invited his actor friends or people he was working with on a particular film. We were invited to join them on occasion. It was particularly fascinating to us whenever he had child actors to the house. When he was filming *Back from Eternity*, he invited Jon Provost, who later starred in the television show *Lassie*. Jon was about four years old and fell asleep on the couch; he was so tiny and cute. The film's leading lady, Anita Ekberg, also was there that evening. I had brought in my little green parakeet, named Mischievous, to show everyone. The little bird flew into the air before landing on Anita's breasts and then immediately dove down between them. She and I had quite a time, to the intense amusement of all the adults, trying to lure it back out. On major holidays, such as Christmas or Easter, my parents threw large catered parties. I was always baffled by how they could have so many friends.

My mother usually came to our nursery in the evenings. On a rare afternoon, she might surprise us by bringing sliced apples with their skins removed or unpeeled oranges with the centers dug out and filled with sugar for us to suck the juice from. In the evenings, we eagerly awaited her arrival, having been bathed, our hair brushed with one hundred strokes, and dressed in matching nightgowns, pajamas, bathrobes, and slippers. It was always a treat. My mother was the object of my devotion, the center of my focus, a goddess to me, magical in every way, engulfing my imagination. Being from Ireland, she was a gifted storyteller. We spent our evenings riveted to her accounts of ethereal lands, and her stories of water babies, mermaids, and fairies.

The worlds she created for us were full of enchanted creatures, both good and bad, and although rarely seen, they often could be sensed. She told us tales so intriguing I remained in those worlds for days afterward. She had us close our eyes and enter these worlds freely. But if we opened them, the shy elves and fairies hid and ran away. I never opened my eyes. We could hear the soft trickle of the flowing brooks, where the fairies bathed and played. If we were very still, they would even climb upon us, play in our hair and jump from our hands. And if we listened very carefully, we could hear their laughter behind the trickle of the streams.

Sometimes, they whispered secrets in our ears, only to be remembered by us while under the spell of the enchanted lands. My mother's stories were so compelling and convincing that she became a part of the bewitchment. Her voice was like no other—melodic, soft, infinitely charming, and irresistible. It resonated with my inner core and somehow spoke to that alone. She sat before us, and as she moved or gestured or looked into our eyes, I could swear sparks emanated from her divine being.

From my perspective, she was a queen fairy. I envisioned her kingdom to be deep in the sea. Her color was mystical green, but she radiated blue light. When she entered the nursery, its everyday decor, which was cozy and warm, was transformed into a place of all possibilities, as if the walls, bureaus, beds, and even our nurse receded, disappearing into space. And suddenly, we were surrounded by rivulets, endless sky, trees, mountains, and fields of flowers, all inhabited by ethereal and illusive gnomes, goblins, elves, and fairies.

NEWBORN PRUDENCE WITH HER
TWO PARENTS IN 1948

NEWBORN PRUDENCE WITH HER
TWO PARENTS AND FOUR OLDER
SIBLINGS IN 1948

LEFT TO RIGHT
JOHNNY, PRUDENCE, MIA,
PATRICK, MAUREEN, STEFFI,
MICHAEL 1950

two

Irish Mother

There was always an air of magic about my mother and her past. As we grew older, she spoke to us about her childhood and family in Ireland. Her grandfather John Lovat Frazer and his family, on her mother's side, had lived in Roscommon in the west of Ireland for centuries. He was a wealthy surgeon, retired from the navy; he had served years at a large hospital in Tientsin, China. He had married an Englishwoman, Eva Mary Kennett. They had eight children, all born in China—four sons followed by four daughters. My mother's mother, our Granny as we called her, was the oldest of those girls. Granny was the only one of my mother's Irish family that we knew, though we briefly met my mother's three younger sisters and their children in Ireland over the summer of 1959, when I was eleven. I now occasionally communicate with some of these first cousins via Facebook.

My mother's Grandfather Frazer was forced to leave China during the Boxer Rebellion (1899-1901) toward the end of the Qing dynasty, and returned to settle in Roscommon on a large family estate called Riversdale. According to my mother, the enormous manor house was made of stone, distinguished by a covering of thick moss and ivy. The house was three stories high with several attics and many rooms. The living room and drawing room were dark and spacious with enormous fireplaces and high ceilings. There was no electricity, so the whole house was lit by lantern and candlelight. My mother told us that when she stayed there, every night after everyone had gone to bed and the house was quiet, her grandfather remained downstairs. She would inevitably hear the resonant sound of the heavy wooden drawing room doors sliding shut behind him as he cloistered himself.

Sometimes sneaking to the top of the staircase, she could see the flickering light of the huge fireplace coming from under the great doors. Then, almost ritually, the muffled sound of the tuning of many instruments would begin. She would then hear her grandfather's voice speaking loudly, as if he were trying to be heard over the chatter of several people. This was followed by eerily exquisite music played by an unearthly orchestra she had never heard before or since. These nightly concerts lasted until the breaking of the first rays of dawn. She tried asking her parents about these gatherings but was admonished for having an overactive imagination. One night, waking her younger brother for courage, she mustered the strength to slip downstairs and knock on the enormous walnut doors during the middle of a late-night session.

At first there was no response, so with her heart in her mouth she knocked louder and more boldly. The music stopped suddenly, and her grandfather opened the dark doors ever so slightly. She later swore she could see in and no one was there. Peering through that crack, he angrily told the two children to return to bed or he would tell their parents about their nighttime prowling. He watched them race back up the stairs. The great doors closed shut. Stopping at the top of the landing just out of sight, my mother listened to her grandfather's muffled voice and the music resumed.

It was no use pestering her father for an explanation, for even if he knew what was going on, he would never give in and tell her, but my mother knew Granny could eventually be broken down.

Finally after numerous requests, Granny told my mother in a most matter-of-fact manner that Grandfather Frazer was what people call a "spiritualist," and the music was coming from the spirits he contacted and worked with in the evenings. She added that "spiritualism" runs in the family and that an earlier ancestor was apparently very well-known in certain circles for his nightly musical soirees. Now, my mother was told she must promise not to ask any more about it.

Granny's mother, my great-grandmother Eva, was a socialite and *bon vivant* who spent much of her time at gambling casinos in Monte Carlo and Italy. She and Grandfather Frazer separated when they returned to Ireland from China—she was in charge of the four girls, and he raised the four boys. She divided her time between several of their homes. The way Granny told it, her mother was a beautiful and headstrong woman who smoked thin cigars, preferred the company of men, and loved gambling and drinking. All four girls, including my Granny, were devoted to their mother.

Granny's proud Irish family considered themselves aristocrats and believed they were superior to almost all others. They enjoyed one another so much that, as Granny put it, they never felt the need for anyone else's company. Granny's father's family had been wealthy for many centuries, with sprawling estates throughout Roscommon and western Ireland. And although the O'Sullivan family she married into was perhaps wealthier than her own, Granny always felt she had married beneath herself by marrying an O'Sullivan. Even though her husband's father had been Lord Mayor of County Cork and knighted for charity work, they would always remain merchants who made their money selling butter and feather beds.

Granny was considered an Irish beauty. My mother described her as a will-o'-the-wisp whose constantly changing interests were banal in the eyes of her poor husband. She had inherited her mother's good looks and proud sense of superiority, causing her to feel out of place among others until the day she died. Upon the death of her mother and premature deaths of two younger sisters, she grew more remote, reiterating that she would never find anyone as fascinating and entertaining as her own kin. The only reason she had married, she explained, was because she was the victim of a compelling "vision" that had cursed her to live a life for which she had little interest. Gradually, she took to the bottle to drown her misery. My mother always insisted it was not drink that was the ruin of her but rather sheer boredom.

One day, Granny told my mother exactly why she had married her husband, my grandfather. She was seventeen and going, as was usual for her family, to play tennis with her brothers and sisters at the private club near their home. All her brothers were soldiers belonging to the Connaught Rangers, an Irish regiment of the British army. When she arrived this particular afternoon, she heard that several young soldiers home on leave were visiting the club. After lunching and changing into her tennis outfit, she arrived at the courts with one of her sisters, who casually mentioned that the two strangers on the other side of the net had invited them to a game.

As she looked across the court and saw the pair of young men facing her, her eyes could not help but focus on the young soldier directly opposite her. He was smiling at her and, clearly, had been watching her for some time. She felt almost annoyed, thinking he had nerve displaying such an arrogant grin, when suddenly an uncontrollable and overwhelming flash of intuition blazed before her eyes—this was the man she would marry! She felt faint, dizzy, and disconnected all at once, but there was no denying it; she was certain this marriage would come to pass and nothing could prevent it from happening. When he crossed the net to introduce himself, she, without even realizing, found herself boldly declaring, "You are the man I will marry."

Charles Joseph O'Sullivan, my mother's father, would indeed marry her, and their first child was my mother. He had chosen a military career and was a captain in the historical Irish Connaught Rangers, often referred to as "The Devil's Own." The Rangers was an elite regiment, disbanded in 1922 upon formation of the Irish Free State. Because her father spent some years in India, my mother developed an almost obsessive fascination with that country, borne from the exotic tales he told her. Being the oldest of his four children—three girls and a boy—she often served as his closest confidante, especially as her mother's behavior grew more distant and unpredictable. Despite my mother's closeness with her family, she was destined to be their only child to leave Ireland.

It was common in those days for horse-driven caravans of Irish Travellers (Gypsies and Tinkers, as they were once called) to travel along the small dirt country lanes crisscrossing much of Ireland. My mother and her siblings were cautioned, in no uncertain terms, to never speak to them. Once, while playing with her brother in the rolling fields outside their country estate, a Gypsy caravan was spotted in the distance, meandering its way along the bumpy dirt road. My mother, ten at the time, raced across the fields with her brother to get a better view of the colorful caravan. If they were lucky, they might even get to hear them speak their foreign Shelta tongue, the language spoken by the Irish Travellers.

The plan was to dash across to the other side of the lane before the caravan's arrival and hide in the nearby grove of trees. As my mother bolted toward the road, a strange feeling of motionlessness suddenly engulfed her, as if time were suspended. She stopped and turned fearlessly to face the oncoming caravan. Her brother saw her strange behavior and wildly waved, screamed, and tugged at her to run and hide, but she could do nothing, as if her feet were filled with lead. He pulled madly at her one last time before quickly diving for refuge in the grove as the troop neared. My mother reported that everything around her, all motion and sound, slowed to a halt. A calm washed over her as the silence gradually took the form of an old woman's voice whose beckoning echoed gently. The large horses pulled to a stop in front of her, and an old Gypsy woman climbed down from a seat high on top of the tall, colorful, intricately painted wagon.

The old woman was smiling as she walked toward my mother and tenderly lifted her small hands into her own, turning the palms upward. She appeared weary, almost sad. She looked at my mother's upturned hands, her manner warm and intimate. Speaking softly but deliberately, she looked deeply into my mother's eyes and said she had seen her playing in the fields from afar and immediately recognized her as one of her own. This is why she called her. The woman explained that, right now, little of this conversation would make sense to her, but as the years progress, one day she would come to value their meeting. My mother felt removed and distant, as if she were watching this played out for someone else. My mother later concluded that "someone else" was herself. The old Gypsy was speaking past the child to the woman my mother was to become. How many countless times over her lifetime she relived this moment, relying on its mystical power to take her through difficult times.

"You have the heart of a Gypsy, my child," the old woman told her. "No matter what you do, where you live or travel to, this will never change." She went on to predict many major events marking my mother's future life. She told her she would be, at the age of eighteen, the only one of her family to leave Ireland, never to live there again. Placing her withered hands on my mother's head, as if invoking all the forces of heaven, she spoke gravely. "Always remember this meeting and you will find peace in your most challenging moments. You are destined to wander, for the heart of the Gypsy knows no home—everywhere is our home…" There was more, but my mother never told us, for she was sworn to secrecy.

She doesn't know how long their meeting lasted. It could have been ten minutes or several hours. Her brother reported that, as the caravan neared, he ran to her side, yelling and pulling at her several times, but she never moved or responded. He watched safely from behind the nearby trees as the caravan approached. But when the old woman climbed down and walked toward my mother, it took all he had to keep from screaming as he bounded toward the safety of home and help. My mother lingered and watched as the old woman and her caravan faded into the distance. She says she felt helpless, like a baby in the arms of its mother.

My mother returned home just as the family was rushing to her aid. Her brother's version of what happened spurred panic, for the children had been told many times never to speak to Gypsies. My mother was punished and confined to her room for two days.

The distinctive and haunting voice of the Gypsy recurred in her mind, like a sweet lullaby, for many hours later. And she felt a strange inner peace, which lasted for days beyond her brief bedroom confinement.

When recounting this story, she often recited from memory the first verse of a poem by Robert William Service, titled "The Men That Don't Fit In," only she called it "The Gypsies":

There's a race of men that don't fit in,
A race that can't stay still;
So they break the hearts of kith and kin,
And they roam the world at will.
They range the field and they rove the flood,
And they climb the mountain's crest;
Theirs is the curse of they gypsy blood,
And they don't know how to rest...

three

Off to Hollywood

In 1929, when my mother was seventeen (and a half, to be exact), an incident occurred that forever changed her life. After finishing boarding school at Sacred Heart Convent in London and bidding farewell to her classmates—one of whom was the soon-to-be actress Vivian Leigh, star of the movie *Gone With the Wind*—my mother arrived home in Dublin. Met by her parents, she promptly received an invitation from her father to join him in attending a large and prestigious ball. Everyone who was anyone would be there. It was to be my mother's coming-out of sorts, a kind of initiation into adulthood. Almost overwhelmed by excitement, she prepared for the affair. No expense appeared too great; her mother made sure of it. She had her hair done and, for the first time in her life, a manicure and pedicure.

Dublin's best seamstress made her dress, using the most expensive linens and silks available. Her shoes were imported, ordered from London's high-end Harrods department store. Every detail of her grooming was tended to with the utmost of care. She was aware that for Granny, this was an attempt at the completion of many years of training and instilling in her a definitive sense of class superiority. But in the moment, my mother didn't care—it was all too exhilarating.

All her life she had felt she never measured up to the good looks of her mother and grandmother, but this particular evening even she had to admit that she was ravishingly beautiful. Everyone seemed to take notice of her; many were compelled to remark on her striking beauty. Emboldened by this, and perhaps with the help of a few drinks, she began to mingle, confidently flirting like never before. Unfortunately, few people near her age were in attendance. Scanning the spacious ballroom, she spotted a small gathering of young people whose animated activity appeared vibrant and exciting. She nimbly picked her way through the thick crowds.

As she mingled with the younger group, she felt the eyes of someone across the room intently focusing on her. It was American movie director Frank Borzage. He was in Dublin to film a movie titled *Song O' My Heart* starring legendary Irish tenor John McCormack. Borzage worked for William Fox and his Fox Film Corporation (which later merged with Twentieth Century Pictures to become what is now 20th Century Fox). According to my mother, Fox Film executives felt the studio's lead actress Janet Gaynor was asking for too much money, and they were looking to replace her with a new talent. Borzage decided he had found their star, a colleen with long dark-brown curly hair and bright-blue eyes. Her name was Maureen O'Sullivan. She would do a screen test for him and costar in this film while in Ireland. He would then bring her back to America as Fox Film's new star. It took some time, however, before Borzage could convince my grandfather to let my mother leave Ireland and travel to Hollywood.

But once my mother set her mind, there was no stopping her. Although Granny had long touted the glorious qualities of my great-grandmother's female-empowering independence, she grudgingly admitted that when it came to her own daughter's choice to go halfway around the world, she no longer relished such virtues with quite the same fervor. When they saw their daughter's unrelenting pleas of passion, my grandparents knew they had lost her. They reluctantly gave their blessings upon the agreement that Granny would travel to America with her. This was at the insistence of my grandfather, who could not imagine sending a young woman of eighteen so far from her family without a proper chaperone.

As my mother told it, they arrived in America, crossing the Atlantic in the grandest of style on a large ocean liner. No amount of money was spared. They stayed in first-class accommodations, a luxurious suite with large windows overlooking the endless view of sky and sea. They were waited on lavishly with expensive food and beverages (until her death, champagne remained my mother's favorite drink). The studio gave her a large wooden maple walk-in trunk filled with elegant silk gowns, matching shoes and hats, and tailored outfits.

They were met in New York City by press agents, flashing cameras, and crowds, all carefully staged and orchestrated by the studio's publicity arm. The studio was banking on its newest hope. Everything was crafted to create the image of a new star, young Maureen O'Sullivan, a fresh and beautiful Irish girl. They continued traveling by train across the country, stopping at the big cities to be met by more press, flashing cameras, and crowds. But through all the pomp, both my mother and Granny confessed that no matter how intoxicating the glamour and attention were, neither could forget the blinding fact that they would soon walk the same streets, eat at the same restaurants, and even meet many of the same people who once knew recently deceased Rudolph Valentino! He was the silent film industry's mega sensation—the first major male sex symbol and superstar of the burgeoning new moving-picture era. According to my mother, every woman in the world, including her and Granny, was in love with him.

Once they arrived in Hollywood, my mother was given her own furnished house, personal secretary, cook, and servants. Granny stayed with her for several months before returning to Ireland. After completing some final studio shooting in Los Angeles for *Song O' My Heart*, my mother immediately went to work on two other films, *So This Is London* (1930) and *A Connecticut Yankee* (1931), both starring Will Rogers, one of the world's most famous celebrities at that time. But after the release of her first three films, the studio found their Irish star did not capture the hearts of the American public as they had hoped. Soon my mother was moved from her own house into bungalow dormitories reserved for other competing starlets. Her secretary, servants, and cook were dismissed, and she was left to fend for herself.

She was demoted to doing low-budget B movies or, even worse, C-level films, and the studio head suggested she make a trip to visit her family. They arranged everything, and soon she was on her way home, all first-class, once again with her own walk-in trunk. She was greeted in Dublin with a ticker tape parade and enormous crowds proudly proclaiming her as Ireland's own Hollywood star.

She was to stay a few weeks before returning. Toward the end of her visit, she couldn't get through to anyone at the studio and felt a little unsettled. Then a letter came from the studio. It was a bill for her first-class travel home! She couldn't tell anyone. They were all so proud of her, but Ireland would never be the same for her. Scraping her money together, she returned to Hollywood fourth class. She moved in with her Irish film friends and began looking for work. It took a year, the most challenging year of her young life. Then the break came. A friend arranged for her to audition at Metro-Goldwyn-Mayer Studios for the role of Jane in the new *Tarzan the Ape Man* film, and the rest is history.

My mother was one of the more popular ingénues at MGM during the 1930s. For a decade she was Jane Parker opposite Johnny Weissmuller's Tarzan, but she managed to avoid being typecast for that role. Over the course of her career, she made over seventy-five movies, starred in a number of Broadway shows, and appeared in many TV shows. She worked with leading actors of the era, such as William Powell, Myrna Loy, Greta Garbo, Basil Rathbone, Vivien Leigh, Robert Taylor, Lionel Barrymore, and Laurence Olivier. Some of the more widely known films she played in during her heyday at MGM include *The Thin Man* (1934), *Anna Karenina* (1935), *A Yank at Oxford* (1938), and *Pride and Prejudice* (1940). After leaving MGM she appeared in several film noirs directed by my father, the best known being *The Big Clock* (1948) starring Raymond Milland and Charles Laughton.

My mother transitioned into her new American life, happily saying she had always felt somewhat dispossessed from her Irish roots. Upon acclimating to her new life, she finally understood why. How far less complicated Americans seemed. Her perception was that there were no dark secrets, real or imagined, nor the illusive patterns learned from generations of inbred Irish traditions. For the first time in her life, she felt at home with people she had only just met. This trait was true of almost every American she knew.

Their openness struck her more than anything. It was an openness she felt could almost be taken for naïveté if not for a subtle but unmistakable sense of underlying shrewdness, which was easier to ignore than acknowledge. Over time this paradoxical combination grew more unsettling, but somehow it was always held at bay by the overwhelming fusion of friendliness. Still, she preferred treading these waters over those of her homeland. There was something exhilarating about living in America. With the stakes being higher, more to lose, she constantly felt the rush of a gambler. She was addicted to it and, for years, couldn't put her finger on what exactly it was.

One Christmas, while shopping for presents, it hit her. It was the loss of the stifling complexity and inbreeding she left behind in Ireland, the relationship with her past. People lived in the moment here. Everything was always new, with the expectation of more—more of the unknown, a stake in the future. In fact, everyone here was living on the edge, the edge of his or her own reality, forever being upgraded and reshaped by progress. Progress was the modern prophet of this land, spinning at an ever-increasing rate, taking everyone with it, and where it goes nobody knows.

My mother, the movie star, wondered what it would be like to raise children here. The world we would grow up in would be very different from hers, her parents', and that of the many generations before her. Constant change would be so integral to our lives that living without it would be unimaginable. She felt that, although we would look the same as her, her children might as well be a new adaptation to the species—with one foot always in the future.

As time went on, she found she was not alone in this fear. Her American peers, also dismayed by the acceleration of America's fast-paced lifestyle, shared many of her concerns. We, her children, never understood what she was talking about. We grew up with her relying on us to explain the latest gadgets or trends. It was just the natural order of things. For don't children, as stewards of the future, always know more than their parents do?

four

Australian Father

My father, John Farrow, first worked with my mother on the set of *Tarzan Escapes*, the third in the film series, as an unlisted director. Mother was warned by her friends to stay away from him. He had the reputation of being a ladies' man, but she fell madly in love with him and no amount of warning deterred her. Many times my mother clearly conveyed to me that my father was the love of her life. Her first meeting with him was at a large Hollywood party I believe was hosted by renowned stage and film actor Basil Rathbone, most recognized for his film portrayal of Sherlock Holmes (1939–1946), and his wife, Ouida.

The Rathbone parties were legendary. Everybody famous attended them. They were the most enormous, elaborate, expensive parties in all of Hollywood. Although most of these parties were held at their huge mansion in the hills to the east, sometimes they were held at one of the more popular dinner clubs in the Los Angeles area. These often were costume parties with stars competing by wearing the most outlandish and extravagant outfits, dressed as kings, queens, emperors, and noblemen. Otherwise, the attire was very formal with the men in tuxedos and women in elegant evening gowns.

On this particular occasion at the Rathbone home, my mother was dressed in a simple but attractive gown, and could not help but feel intimidated by the magnitude of talent, beauty, and fame surrounding her. Still new to Hollywood, she didn't know many of the party guests and joined a group of lively film people, mostly actors and writers, gathered at one end of the enormous living room near large windows overlooking rolling manicured lawns.

Waiters dressed in crisp black clothing deftly maneuvered their way through the noisy crowds, offering sumptuous trays filled with small steaming dishes of hors d'oeuvres. The sounds of ice jiggling in glasses and pops of champagne corks could be heard behind the soothing music of a small orchestra playing discreetly off to one side of the room.

As she tried to join in with the small lively group of strangers, my mother found their laughter contagious. Eager to participate, she began laughing as well, and people nodded at her and smiled. Her sudden arrival went largely unnoticed, as if she had been there all along. But one stranger noticed. When she looked his way, she saw that he was watching her closely, curiously. She glanced swiftly the other way, pretending she had not seen him. But she had. For a brief moment, their eyes locked and he knew she saw him. And she knew that he knew. In fact, as she described it later, it was as if they were the only two people in the whole room. Everyone else seemed like movie extras.

She tried to continue her game of coyness, but it was futile. He laughed. She couldn't contain herself and laughed, too, so obvious. She would always love that about him, how he so easily saw through her. Although they laughed and joked and talked lightly, they both knew there was something momentous about their meeting. She tried to appear nonchalant, but she knew if it were not for the profound sense of intimacy she felt, she would have been spooked. Why was his presence so utterly captivating as to marginalize everything and everyone else? He triggered some mechanism inside of her that woke her from a phantom existence.

She felt alive for the first time in her life, but the scary part was that she didn't even know this man. Still, it all felt so *right*. As she danced, wrapped in his arms, she knew her destiny was sealed. This was where she belonged, even while a part of her resisted such finality. Wrestling with emotions that appeared irreconcilable, she was afraid of the gravity she felt. For no matter what she thought or said, she had already decided.

He, too, knew fate was intervening the moment he saw her boldly cross the room with such utter abandon. It was as if her heart were wide open for all to see, so it amazed him that no one else in the group noticed her arrival in their midst. He was charmed, watching her adapt to her own obvious invisibility so naturally. He almost laughed out loud when he saw her exchange looks and nod knowingly to conversations she had just minutes earlier joined. But when she glanced his way and they locked gazes, he was certain she had reached deep inside of him, filling him with her spirit. He was enchanted by her and would remain so the rest of his life.

The evening ended far too quickly. My mother had been swept off her feet, in true Hollywood style. She couldn't believe she had found her proverbial Prince Charming but, then again, was she not already living a star-studded fairy tale? The fascinating young man continued to woo her, sending a stream of letters, flowers, and expensive gifts. He visited my mother often during the course of their courtship. She told us how, when they had just begun dating, he came to direct a segment of the early *Tarzan* series, in which she played the iconic lead female role of Jane.

This was during the glam era of the big Hollywood studios of the 1930s through mid-'40s. MGM, producer of the early *Tarzan* films, was the largest of the studios, churning out fifty films a year at its peak, one every nine days. Referring to its A-list movie stars, it billed itself as having "more stars than are in heaven." With a permanent staff of as many as four thousand handling up to twelve thousand actors a day, its empire spread over nearly two hundred acres with six separate lots that housed offices, almost thirty sound stages, several laboratories, special effects units, a music department with one of the world's largest libraries, a lumber mill, an electrical plant, a railroad line, small cities and towns depicting different periods filled with mansions, swimming pools, stables, frontier homes, lakes, a stone bridge, and even a zoo that was home to elephants, lions, monkeys, and more.

Lot 3 alone, where the *Tarzan* movies were shot, was sixty-five acres. The studio built a set dubbed Jungle Island for the series. My mother's description of it was amazing. She said the studio created an actual African jungle planting every kind of tropical foliage imaginable, even bringing in huge trees and filling them with monkeys and other wild creatures for authenticity. Streams were dug throughout, one large and quick, flowing like a river. The man-made lake at the southern end of the "island" required sixty-three million gallons of water to fill. I often wondered if Walt Disney got his initial idea for Disneyland from visits to these sets.

As a young director, my father oversaw a scene on Lot 3 in Jungle Island in which Jane crossed a treacherous body of water. He teased her by making her stand for long periods in the warm tepid waters of the studio-built stream, knowing she hated doing that scene since rumor had it the stream was used by studio workers as an easy-access, makeshift urinal.

Eventually, my mother brought her beau to Ireland to meet her parents. Granny did not like him much and felt it beneath her daughter to marry an Australian. My grandfather, although not thrilled with his daughter's choice, just wanted her to be happy. Both parents worried he was too much of a dreamer, that his ambitions as a Hollywood screenwriter and film director might inhibit his ability to properly support their daughter throughout the years to come. My poor mother became like a miserable cat in heat. Her parents had done everything to dampen the pace and intensity of the relationship, but they quickly realized the futility of their efforts. My mother felt she could no longer exist without John, and he obviously felt the same.

My father embraced his American dream with such iron-grip fervor that, unlike our mother, he left no room for his past. I never heard him even once mention his childhood, family, or life in

Australia. It was not that he didn't speak of his history, for he relished telling us tales of his adventures at sea as a young sailor or stories from his two and a half years in Tahiti. But we heard *nothing* of his childhood. We never knew of our Australian cousins until decades after my father died. Perhaps the strangest thing of all was that we never noticed this vacuum. We never thought it strange, or questioned or wondered why, until years after his death when it was too late to ask him.

In my teens, right after my father died in 1963, I found an old box full of my mother's diaries and other personal papers. One folder consisted of correspondence between her and the aunt who raised my father. In the letters, my great-aunt described a sensitive bright boy who loved reading history and literature. It was clear from her description that, although our father was a romantic and a dreamer, he was also very much a realist. He was ambitious and clearly believed he was destined for more.

Born on February 10, 1904, in Sydney, Australia, my father lost his mother when he was very young. She died in some kind of sanitarium, and it is not clear what killed her. His father's sister, the maiden aunt, raised him and his first cousin, a girl two years younger, the daughter of another aunt who had more children than she could care for.

Father left home to actualize his ambitions at the young age of fifteen, enlisting in the Australian Merchant Navy and living in Tahiti for two years writing two novels (only one, *When Laughter Ends*, was published) before reaching America in the early 1920s. Eventually he arrived on the Hollywood scene as an actor, worked as a writer, and moved into directing. But although he became a successful producer and director, he remained most proud of being a writer.

My father's heading-for-Hollywood storyline begins in San Francisco when he was eighteen years old, a sailor fresh from the sea with big dreams. One evening he went to a popular but small experimental theater to see the play *Hamlet*, but before the curtain was raised, it was announced that the play had to be canceled because the lead actor was ill. My father, with his heavy Australian accent, stood up and shouted, "I can play that role!" He proceeded backstage only to reappear onstage in full costume to act the part completely from memory. His performance was all in good fun and well received by the small but appreciative group of spectators. As the story goes, John Huston was in the audience and found Hamlet-with-an-Australian-accent so hilarious that he befriended my father and invited him down to Hollywood to join him in acting and writing screenplays.

My father soon established himself as a notable screenwriter for DeMille Productions, Paramount Pictures, and RKO Radio Pictures. He made his directorial debut in 1937 with the film *Men in Exile* for Warner. In 1942, he was nominated for an Academy Award as best director for Paramount's *Wake Island*. He went on to direct many successful films starring such notable actors as Alan Ladd, Ray Milland, Edward G. Robinson, John Wayne, Robert Mitchum, and Charles Laughton, to name merely a few.

When not on movie sets, he was writing books, conducting research of some sort, or working through the night on drafting or refining the next script. He loved history and philosophy, and he had a large library that covered several walls with collected works on every topic. Upon marrying my mother, he converted to Catholicism. This required his annulling a previous marriage that had ended in divorce, and from which he had a daughter. This was always a point of contention for our half sister as she grew older, but the conversion in faith had a profound effect on my father. In some ways, he adopted a "born again" approach, and many of his closest friends were Jesuit priests.

My father authored several religious books, his best-known work borne from his life in Tahiti. The bed he slept in while living there had once been that of the leper Father Damien. This naturally piqued his interest, providing impetus for the book, a seminal work on the life of the priest, titled *Damien the Leper*, published in 1937. The publication brought attention to a little-known missionary who, partly because of the book, is now acknowledged as a saint by the Catholic Church. Until recently it was required reading at all Jesuit high schools. Father also published a history of the papacy, titled *Pageant of the Popes,* in 1943, and a biography, *The Story of Sir Thomas More,* in 1956.

My father loved the sea. I've never seen anyone so thoroughly transformed by close proximity to water. He loved swimming, and he made us swim, breaststroke only, far out past the Malibu breakers. My mother was terrified as we often headed out in rough seas well into the waters at elementary-school ages. The bigger the waves, the more we were told to swim full throttle toward them and dive deep as they broke. To retreat from a breaking wave was to face the peril of being caught in its rolling undertow.

I remember heading into huge twenty-foot waves as fast as I could to avoid being tossed and dragged under, and then surfacing on the other side only to once again face the onslaught of another layer of large oncoming waves toward which I was again to swim full throttle with my heart in my throat. As a result of all this swimming out into the large breakers, one might peg me as an avid swimmer. Not quite. Instead, I absorbed the tension of our mother screaming and developed a particularly acute sense of fear when swimming in the ocean.

My father had an Australian friend, Michael Pate, who acted in many of Father's movies and was later a film director in his own right. He and Michael often met early in the morning to swim, all day long, not returning until late in the evening. Our beach house was one of the earliest-built homes in the Malibu Colony. The front part overlooking the water was on stilts, and sometimes during storms, the water lapped violently under the house. We watched from the stilt porch as their heads became tinier and tinier, disappearing over the horizon. They both were fearless, even of sharks. My father taught us to hit the water in a way that deterred the fanged and sharp-finned fish. He showed us how, if this didn't stop them, to hit them on the nose.

He often described dodging the hazards of working in the movie business as far more treacherous than swimming in dangerous shark-infested waters. He strived hard to financially support us; in the '50s, more and more filming moved overseas to offset increased costs of American labor. My father bravely filmed some of the largest battle scenes for any Western movie made. It starred John Wayne and was titled *Hondo* (1953). Although some of the filming was in Mexico, it was one of the last big-budget films to be shot primarily in the United States.

Huge battle scenes requiring thousands of extras could be shot abroad at less than half the US price. As the unions moved into the movie business, the salaries for the compensation of thousands of extras went way up. Of course this was a good thing as it allowed people to provide for their families, but it was challenging for our family as my father, to his dismay, spent increasing time away from us to shoot in distant locations all over the world. During the mid-'50s, for the good part of two years, he worked on *Around the World in Eighty Days*. He directed most of the film but removed his final credit after a disagreement with producer Michael Todd. He was credited for the screenplay and shared an Academy Award for best screenplay with James Poe and S. J. Perelman.

My father returned from his foreign travels bearing all kinds of amazing items we had never seen before. After returning from the Middle East, he recounted vivid stories of men cloaked in long traditional garments performing a "sword dance" and described women mysteriously covered in veils. He befriended King Saud of Saudi Arabia, who gave him a white silk *gutra*, a large square of cloth worn as a headdress, along with a special *igal*, the cord that holds the *gutra* in place, woven with real gold. He brought back an arsenal of fancy weaponry, from swords of every shape and size to ancient guns with gold- and jewel-inlaid handles. I remember being conscious, for the first time, of feeling left out. Everything important in the world seemed to involve only men. I told my father I wanted to someday travel the globe, like he did. He responded that the world was far too dangerous a place for women to travel.

Although Father was usually away working, I felt he had a special gift few of my peers' parents seemed to have. He could make each of his children feel special and entirely loved. I never felt a jealous tinge that he might love another sibling more than he loved me, even though I was fifth in a line of seven. Once when I was a little older, around thirteen, I decided to test his love for me.

One evening I put on my pajamas and went into his room to spend some time with him. His bedroom was separate from my mother's bedroom and arranged like a den with bookcases lining the walls. I sat on his bed while we talked; he was lying on his side with his legged curled up and his upper body propped on pillows. A call came in, so I lay down while he was on the phone. When he finished the call, he thought I had gone to sleep so he began to read. His legs were cramped up, but I watched as he persevered for fear of disturbing me. I wanted to see how long he would last. He stayed a long time, and I believe he would have remained in that crunched-up position the whole night had I not been the one to finally move. I never forgot that.

John Farrow & Maureen O'Sullivan at Hollywood Party in early 1930s

five

Childhood Antics: Growing Up in Beverly Hills

The stability of everyday people in our lives was anchored by a governess and a cook. Our governess was a Scottish nurse, Barbara Dow, who took care of us on and off from the time I was born. Every year or two, complaining of overwork, she argued with my mother and left for several months. But she always came back. She loved us and adored our father, who teased her and made her laugh. She said she didn't want to leave him with a burden.

Barbara was small and compact, with short brown-dyed curly-permed hair. Her lovely soft cocker-spaniel eyes turned instantly into the fierce piercing eyes of an eagle when we were caught misbehaving. But we loved her dearly. The soft folds of skin that hung loosely from her neck and chin fascinated us. Barbara was liberal politically and did all she could to instill in us what she perceived as correct values. Her influence runs deep to this day, as many of my more populist views can be traced back to her.

She constructed the architecture of my world around the concept of "cozy." Cozy is the most ideal state of existence and has come to mean absolute perfection for me. Heaven is a *cozy* place.

Under Barbara's purview, the cornerstone of life back then was coziness, which meant getting bathed, putting on clean nightgowns and slippers, having our hair brushed with one hundred strokes, and sipping a hot chocolate before climbing into bed and falling into a deeply satisfying slumber after a full day of play.

Our cook was a remarkable black woman from Louisiana named Marcel. She was very lovely with glowing skin and, as beautiful as she was outwardly, she was just as much so inwardly. She always had a smile on her face, filled with so much life that it radiated and you could feel it all around her. All of us loved just being near her. When she laughed, which she did often, it came from her core and touched ours—even if it was a little insignificant chuckle, everyone had to laugh along with her. Her heart was so full, and she taught by her example.

She rarely got angry and, if she did, it was always over quickly. I was always amazed that she had six children of her own. She seemed so much younger than our mother, but her oldest child Betty was slightly older than my oldest brother Michael. Her husband did odd jobs around the house and grounds. He taught me to play my first piano tune. Marcel had a son my age, and I was fascinated because he had the name Monroe, as in Marilyn. Occasionally, we saw her children around the grounds but never really played with them. They were either helping their father around the grounds or waiting on their father as he dropped something off.

Marcel was the children's cook, while my mother and father had a separate kitchen and cook, an attractive quick-witted Irish woman named Eileen. Her food was far more elegant and spicy than ours. We never ate it, but we could tell by the smell and look of it. Marcel's meals were made under our mother's careful eye and were very simple but delicious. My favorite meal of hers consisted of cream of mushroom soup, with peas and tuna fish added, poured over white rice. We had it every week for years, since as Catholics we couldn't eat meat on Fridays. Marcel's cooking was so good that she could later boast she was Bob Hope's cook.

All of the female "help" staff wore white nurse-like uniforms, with the exception of Eileen who wore a much fancier black dress with a crisp white apron. Our governesses lived with us while the rest of the help, such as Marcel, came in to work daily. Male workers, such as Marcel's husband, the gardener, and Joe, did not wear uniforms. Joe was a kind black man who drove us to and from school. He also shined my father's and brother's shoes. He worked for my father in the other part of the house, so I'm not sure what else he did.

Besides the solid presence of Marcel and Barbara, a slew of helpers or minor characters came and went in our lives. There was Mary Red-Socks, who always wore colored socks, mostly red or pink. Mrs. Pottage was with us for one of Barbara's longer leaves of absence when I was about seven or eight. Her hair was dyed reddish-blond, worn parted on the side, hinting at covering one eye, wavy and flowing halfway to her shoulders. Although she was going for Marilyn Monroe, she actually looked more like Ethel Merman with a tan (and devoid of personality). She was rather plump with an inordinately large behind. In our backyard, we had wooden rope lounge chairs. It was summertime, and in the afternoon, she sat with us in the yard, doing her needlepoint as we played on the lawn under the sprinklers. Her bottom entirely filled the sturdy chair, bulging out like bread dough through the spaces between the ropes.

One day while Johnny, Steffi, and I were playing, we noticed this and wondered if in fact Mrs. Pottage were wearing an artificial bottom. Somehow this seemed a highly plausible explanation; we needed no further convincing and became fascinated by the novelty of it. It never occurred to us as to *why* she might wear an artificial bottom, so we focused instead on how. We spent almost the entire bright sunny summer afternoon in endless argument and discussion on the subject. Was it strapped on? Did it cover the entire area? If so, how did she go to the bathroom? How thick was it? We decided to test it.

We took turns crawling under her chair, while the others distracted her. We tried to keep her preoccupied by running rapidly around the lawn between the sprinkler and her chair. Each of us took a turn, diving under Mrs. Pottage and poking her behind, while the others asked questions or performed feats of physical wonderment such as somersaults, headstands, and cartwheels. It was quite a maneuver to get under her, for the lounge chairs were low to the ground. We had to not only crawl under but also then turn over without knocking her.

We each went for two tries. My first time, angled sideways since I was unable to fully turn around, I pushed on Mrs. Pottage's bum with one probing finger. She did not notice. By our second round, we'd all learned that turning over just before going under the chair and proceeding on our backs cut the time in half. Still, she did not notice. We were convinced her bum was artificial, but we needed a definitive inspection. She had her sewing basket at her side, and we managed to get hold of a pin. It was getting late, we were running out of diversionary tactics, and we needed to act quickly. Since I was particularly skilled at the diving-and-turning move, I was nominated for this last mission. I dove under and stuck the pin almost all the way in. There was *no* reaction from her. Our decision was final: we were certain she had an artificial behind at least two inches thick.

I imagined it made of rubbery plastic, slightly coarse in texture, much like the material two of our dolls were made of. The dolls belonged to me and Steffi (I think Mia had one too). Mine was an infant, and Steffi's was a toddler. They both were very lifelike. Their skin had a strange texture, a mixture that was soft and yet buoyant due to what appeared to be just the right consistency of rubber and plastic. I attributed it to being very high-tech and modern. No other dolls had skin like this, and I was convinced Mrs. Pottage's artificial bottom must be made of the same material.

Each doll had come with a kind of suitcase that opened up, and on one side were matching outfits on little plastic hangers while the other held more utilitarian necessities. In my case, this consisted of a baby bottle that could be filled with water, pull-up diapers, booties, and pajamas. Steffi's doll had a hairbrush, comb, three colorful small plastic barrettes, and a pair of black patent-leather shoes. I kept my doll secretly hidden under my bed for fear of having to face relentless teasing by my older brother Patrick, who thought playing with dolls was for sissies and crybabies.

My fascination with my doll became almost a fetish for me. I secretly took her out from under the bed at night when no one could see me feeding her and dressing her in different outfits and booties. I felt ashamed about the pleasure this gave me, but I was unable to resist it. Steffi's way of dealing with this need was far more clever. She got our mother to buy her tiny little dolls she could fit in her pocket and secretly play with on the sly.

Mrs. Pottage swam in the afternoons while we napped and rested. Our swimming pool was very private, surrounded by a high fence shrouded in ivy and foliage of all kinds. Word about her artificial bottom got around the neighborhood, and some of the older children wanted more proof. So one afternoon, while she was changing into her clothes after swimming, Mia and Patrick climbed up a tree near the fence and took pictures, which all of us later inspected. I still remember them now—her behind did not look fake. She was very plump. The pictures were taken from a distance with a little Brownie camera, so they were blurred enough to leave some doubt in our minds.

One hot evening at bedtime, Steffi and I decided to investigate further. Mrs. Pottage, wearing her pink shorty nightgown, exercised in the evenings before bedtime in our large bedroom, which at this age I shared with Steffi and Tisa. Performing what appeared to be a dance, Isadora Duncan–style, this nightly ritual took place in the spacious open area in front of our beds. We paid no attention, as usual. Once lights were out, Mrs. Pottage went into the bathroom we shared with her, just off of our bedroom. Her smaller bedroom was down the hall.

Steffi and I met quietly in the dark of our bedroom and crept silently over to the door of the bathroom. It was wide open. She was bent over the sink, brushing her teeth in that pink nightie. We crawled stealthily over, and peering upward, I remember that sight to this day. As the night sky is marked by its patterns of stars, the massive area that was Mrs. Pottage's backside was punctuated with innumerable dimples, like fingerprints. Steffi called it "cottage cheese." Amazed, and as if in a trance, I mindlessly reached up to put my fingers in the indentations. Fortunately Steffi stopped me, and we quickly scurried back to our beds undetected by Mrs. Pottage. That night, the myth of the artificial bottom was finally put to rest.

Another memorable fill-in nanny for Barbara was Mrs. Person. She came just after Mrs. Pottage, when I was still eight. She was a brittle strict black woman, and we did not care much for her. We were always in trouble with her, and she took a branch from the willow tree, calling it a "switch," and whipped it across our naked behinds. It stung badly. My mother finally caught on. Mrs. Person left, and my mother begged Barbara to return.

Barbara did not come back right away, and we had Lucille for a year and a half. Lucille, unlike the other nannies, did not live with us full-time, only staying during the week and returning on the weekend to her home, where she lived with her Aunt Nettie. Lucille often brought us to her home to visit. Her aunt owned an enormous green parrot named Bill, who could say, "Hello, baby," and, "I love you, baby." Lucille called Tisa her "baby doll." I was entranced by Bill. He had the clear deep voice of a male, almost like an actor's. I just couldn't get over how that articulate adult voice came out of Bill's large orange beak.

During the summers all the neighborhood children ran wild like a pack of wolves. I remember running and running as the older children shouted and screamed commands for hours on end until dusk set in. We played traditional backyard games, such as hide-and-seek (or its variant, Sardines), Red Rover, and Mother May I. Each neighboring home's privacy was staked out, surrounded by large trees and spacious yards. The neighbors next door were legendary film producer Hal Roach and his family.

Hal Roach is best known for producing the now-classic Laurel and Hardy and *Our Gang* (later commonly known as *The Little Rascals*) comedy film series. He was considered a visionary ahead of his time, the first big film producer to move into television. In the '50s, his studio produced many popular shows, such as *My*

Little Margie, The Gale Storm Show, Racket Squad, The Stu Erwin Show (sometimes referred to as *The Trouble with Father*), and others that pioneered American sitcoms.

Mrs. Roach was a good friend to my parents, and their three girls were the same age as Tisa, Steffi, and I. We were even in the same grades at the same schools. Their home was palatial and, by far, the best place to play. The winding driveway curved deeply into their densely wooded property and back around again. Near the end of the long driveway, just before it circled back, was a cavernous four-car garage set below a huge colonial house, a separate structure that provided living quarters for the servants. Sometimes we played with the servants' children, who lived on the property. One girl Mia's age was from Russia, and she could jump rope longer and faster than we ever thought possible. Another was a boy whose parents had escaped from Hungary—he was always playing pranks. His most memorable feat was his ability to throw a ball so high into the air that it seemed to disappear in the sky. This amazed all of us, even the older kids.

The Roach family home, the main house, was halfway down the curvy driveway lined with thick stands of pine trees on both sides. The expansive front lawn was laced with large scattered magnolias. Inside, the colonial-style mansion provided an endless source of imaginative play. Two large columns facing into the living room framed a huge marble hallway, perfect for staging our plays, neighborhood extravaganzas such as *Peter Pan, Cinderella,* and *My Fair Lady,* as well as our own pieces.

Hal Roach had an enormous downstairs den, paneled in dark wood, with leather furniture and a movie projector. This is where he viewed films and where we saw many of his first projects, like *Babes in Toyland* and the old comedy classics starring Stan Laurel and Oliver Hardy. The walls were filled with pictures of influential people gathered together at racetracks, on a polo field, around pool tables, and in nightclubs and gambling halls. A section of Hal's underground lair had a colossal bearskin on the floor, complete with snarling head and baring teeth; a giant moose head peered from the wall above the large stone fireplace. When we played in this room and turned out the lights, it turned pitch-black, and we could not hope to see even our hands in front of our eyes. Needless to say, this was the older children's favorite haunt as they could scare us younger ones out of our living wits.

The Roach estate's gardens were finely manicured around a central Olympic-size blue-tile pool with wonderful hand-painted sea creatures spread about. When we dove off the diving board into the deep end of the pool, we jetted into the tentacles of a massive gray octopus painted on the tiles at the bottom. Each side of the pool was flanked by a garden with fountains and ponds stocked with goldfish. Two bathhouses sat at the back of the pool, one on each side.

One bathhouse was a big game-room facility, one of our favorite places. It was furnished with several beautiful large wooden billiards and card tables, with stacks of brand-new packages of playing cards underneath. Every time we went in, we each opened our own new pack of cards—that always felt and smelled so good. The walls were lined with tall glass and wooden cases filled with trophies and awards mostly from polo games.

The other bathhouse was where the family enjoyed saunas and received massages—the mother of the Russian girl who could jump rope so well was the masseuse for a while. The roof of the massage house was perfect for a fort, which we used regularly and called the "Kiki." Our fort overlooked the tennis court situated behind the pool. The lined surface of the tennis court was perfect for our roller-skating competitions. Off to the side of the make-shift skate rink was a lovely rose garden. It was fascinating, full of the most exotic caterpillars, which we would play with and collect.

Agreeably the favorite hangout for everyone in the neighborhood was on the Roach property's exterior grounds. We called it the "Big Tree," and it was the best climbing tree. It seemed at any given point during the day, someone was up in that tree—and it was not a children-only area. My parents called it the "Thinking Tree." Sometimes on warm summer evenings, they sat, having cocktails, high up on its lower swooping branch. It was the delight and dream of any child or tree climber. It had wonderful stages to it, providing terrific stopping points on the way up. The path up wound around the massive and wondrous trunk, circling it even as it thinned all the way to the top. About midway, there was one very precarious spot that weeded out the courageous from the cowardly—hindering me for a long while. It required circling the trunk while stepping across from one branch to the other with nothing to hold onto. We pressed our bodies against the trunk, with our arms attempting to stretch around it—only it was too wide to grasp.

At the beginning of the climb was a wonderful large fat branch that gracefully and in an easy manner swept out from the tree like the bare swayed back of a farm horse. It was very broad, and we could lie there resting and look far up to the top of the tree. It was wonderful for daydreaming. We called it the "Bed." At one point, Mrs. Roach forbade her children to climb the tree. She complained to my parents about how dangerous it was for children. One evening she came out to the Big Tree, furious to find her children roaming around its large base. Looking up in horror, she saw my parents resting leisurely on the Bed over cocktails. She let out a scream at the sight, but couldn't resist a laugh as my father charmingly invited her to join them. We all loved Mrs. Roach.

The Big Tree was benevolent, like a grandfather or old sage. It must have reached ten stories high. Crouching at its uppermost top branches, we were rocked from side to side as it swayed and creaked in the wind. High up there, we could see for great distances large swaths of land and rolling hills.

Life went on happily for us, just as it was—running wild until evening in our flannel shirts, blue jeans, and PF Flyers lace-up sneakers, and then to bed early. Bedtime was 6:30 p.m. until I was eight, and then it was increased a half-hour to seven. The first question I usually asked other children was what time they went to bed. There was always an aura of great intrigue about how late they got to stay up. It somehow seemed to tell me a lot about them. Barbara had successfully ingrained in us that going to bed early would keep us healthy and younger as we grew up. We were by far in bed the earliest of all the other children, not only in the neighborhood but that I had ever known. I felt a secret pride in this. I pitied all the children I played with, when I looked at what I thought were darkening shadows under their eyes, confirmation to me of the early signs of aging—and they didn't even know any better.

My only real awareness of being a famous Hollywood family was when tourist buses regularly passed by our house. We heard them coming well in advance, with loudspeakers blaring out the names of the stars. On our block were singing comedian Jimmy Durante, beautiful actress Eleanor Parker, beloved entertainer Jack Benny, two Marx brothers, and some well-known producers. When we heard a bus coming, the neighborhood children raced out to the street and performed all kinds of dramatizations, such as acting out violent scenes with our cap guns going off loudly, pretending to punch one another and falling to the ground as we had seen on our fathers' movie sets, hugging one another to mimic a love scene, making horrible faces, standing on our heads, riding on the backs or shoulders of one another, dancing wildly, and jumping rope. All of this was punctuated by screams and loud laughter. One day as the bus passed our way with its speaker blaring, we got particularly wild and someone pulled down his pants for all on the bus to see. This was reported to our parents, and it was a long time before we were again allowed out front when the buses came down the street.

JOHNNY, PRUDENCE AND MIA AS
THREE COWBOYS 1951

Lt to rt - Prudence, Johnny,
Mia, Patrick, Michael 1951

Johnny, Eileen holding baby
Steffi and Prudence, and Mia
1950

six

Influences and Undercurrents

We attended the local parochial school, where not all students were Catholic. It was filled with children of the era's well-known stars, including the offspring of Lucy and Desi Arnaz, Dean Martin, Ricardo Montalban, Jeanne Crain, and Betty Grable. Their parents enrolled them there because it was considered one of the better grammar schools in the area. They couldn't have anticipated the subtle trauma it would inflict on the tender psyches of their children. One of my close classmates was Protestant, which meant she was not allowed to receive Holy Communion or any of the sacraments, including confession, the sole means for forgiveness of sins according to Catholicism.

Every day, school began with an hour of religion class. We were taught that those who were not baptized could not enter heaven and were sent to a place called "Limbo," where they could never see God and would be neither happy nor sad. My friend was baptized, so we felt relieved that at least she did not have to go to Limbo (although we weren't completely sure). We could not imagine what she felt when excluded from Holy Communion. Even as children, the subject was too sensitive for us to broach. She never mentioned it, but she did tell us she went to another church and received communion.

As I stated at the beginning of this book, I counted down with dread from four years old until I was to reach six, the age of reason, which meant I was responsible for all my thoughts and actions and could go to hell. I remember the pity I felt for Mia and Johnny when they reached the age of reason. It would soon be my turn, and there was nothing I could do about it—it was inevitable. As my sixth birthday drew near, my fear and trepidation grew. I was terrified, feeling completely alone. Even though I knew reaching the age of reason was a rite of passage from childhood to adulthood—everyone did it—this gave me no comfort. As time ticked away, I spent many hours in serious thought on the Bed of the Big Tree, trying to calm myself down. It was a place of solace where I, like my parents, could go to think. But rather than feeling soothed, I felt profoundly sobered. One day I solemnly came to the somber conclusion that I was as old as I would ever be.

An entire year of religion classes was spent in preparation for first Holy Communion. In the months leading up to it, whole days were carved out of each week for rehearsals as we practiced the procession up the center aisle of the church with the shortest students leading in front and the tallest in the back. The boys formed their own line on the right. Excitedly, we all went shopping for white Communion dresses, shoes, gloves, and veils. Each of us received a special prayer book we would keep our whole lives. We were photographed individually and as a group. It was the high point of our collective existence as second-graders. In the years to follow, every first Friday of the month, the whole class would fast for Holy Communion, receiving hot chocolate and donuts for breakfast afterward.

I viewed my Holy Communion as a consolation gift from God for having passed into the dreaded age of reason. It seemed to be the one happy moment in an otherwise dark and frightening series of rites and realizations. Holy Cross Order ran our school, with all the classes taught by nuns. Their religious habits were made up of the usual black garb with large crucifixes tied at their waists and large hooded "halos" of white encircling their faces. To this day, it is nearly impossible to imagine them as everyday women with hairstyles.

The weapons of Catholicism at that time were lethal. There was an obsession in our religion classes with sin and Satan. Reaching the age of reason meant I was responsible for not only every action but also every thought, such as wanting to see the nuns without their habits. The perceived devastation brought on by my own mistakes weighed heavily. I practically begged my second-grade religion teacher for some kind of escape clause that would allow me an out on my thoughts. Unequivocally, the answer came back: thoughts are as bad as the actions themselves. I knew I was a lost cause.

I lived from weekly confession to weekly confession, praying that if I had to die to let it be right after confession. Although my religion classes spoke about the love of God, it was always eclipsed by explanations of sin and the devil. We were taught two principal categories of sin. First, there were major sins, called mortal sins—anything to do with sex, for instance. Then there were minor sins, called venial sins—mean thoughts, as an example. The consequence in the afterlife, which seemed to be the main concern, was purgatory for venial sins or hell for mortal sins. Purgatory was as bad as hell, only it was temporary.

As conveyed by the nuns, the agony of hell was truly the most formidable of all possible imaginings. The worst part of which was being cut off from God, forever. I didn't quite understand how being cut off from God could be worse than the eternal fires of hell, but I took the sisters at their word. We were warned not to think that purgatory was any better just because it wasn't for all eternity. I remember one nun trying to help us conceive of eternity. She brushed her fingers lightly over the wall of our classroom. She said if she were to do this once a year every year until all the walls in the classroom and building were rubbed away, this would merely be one moment in eternity. Immediately, I thought of purgatory, where one is sentenced to many moments, such as ten minutes, a half day, one day, ten days, three months, or a year—who needed to think of hell? My fears were immeasurable. Hours of my thinking and conceptualizing as a little girl were engrossed in these concepts.

Of course, hell wouldn't be complete without the concept of "the devil." Many nights I lay in my bed, staring out into the vast darkness surrounding me and praying out loud to the devil to stay away. The nuns made sure we were cornered on both accounts. If you were bad, the devil would possess you, and if you were very good, the devil would come to test you. The sight of even the smallest speck of him was so inconceivably horrible that one went mad. The nuns told us several tales of people who did not survive such a sight. But one priest did live. The story goes that the priest had been praying for a man whose soul was turning to badness. The devil was fighting to possess the man, and came banging at the priest's door to stop him from praying for this soul. The priest kept praying. The devil then entered his room. The priest knew he should keep praying, but in weakness, he turned and looked at him. The devil looked like an average man except for a clubbed left foot. As soon as the priest saw the foot, he went mad and all his hair turned white. He never recovered.

The devil made a perceived visitation to Mia, and it took me years to recover from that. It was late at night, and she and I shared the same room. She woke me with a hoarse whisper, as she lay paralyzed in terror. I climbed into bed with her. She said he stood over her and was now looking through the glass window of the kitchen door into our bedroom, lit by a night-light. "Do you see his dark figure looming behind the glass?" she asked me.

I absorbed her terror. "Yes, I see some figure, dark and utterly hideous!" I whispered back. I saw a shadowy shape move away from the window. For days she wrote about the incident in her diary, showing it to Barbara, our parents, and the nuns. Meantime, I was engulfed by a fear that only grew because he had stood by my bed before hers!

We were taught, "The family that prays together stays together." Nightly, after my mother's stories, we knelt on prayer benches before a statue of Our Lady, the Blessed Virgin Mary, built into a tiny alcove in the wall in the hallway to my parents' quarters. We said a decade of the rosary—one Our Father and ten Hail Marys. We took turns reciting each night. On Sundays, we did a full rosary, five decades.

The third great preoccupation of my childhood, besides hell and the devil, was war. These were the peak years of America's Cold War with Russia, which shadowed our everyday existence. I frequently had vivid nightmares of communists invading our town, running through our streets and backyards, shooting and trying to break into homes.

Once every month on a Friday, the atmosphere was hit with the harsh bizarre sound of air-raid sirens going off all over the city for a bomb drill. It was an eerie sound, not anything like the clang of a fire alarm or the whirling sounds of an ambulance on its way to help someone. Its harshness instilled not the comfort of rescue but instead the helpless fear associated with the potentiality of being hit with an H-bomb for which we inherently knew any preparation was ludicrous. Still, as soon as the alarm sounded, we obediently dove under our school desks, crouching and putting our hands over our heads as directed until we were told all was clear. After it stopped, we laughed and clowned around, but during these drills, we were dead silent.

Despite our outward denial combined with a pervasive entertainment culture that smothered children with Disney-esque happy endings, in contrast we secretly harbored a disproportionate sense of dread. Television specials discussing war were aired often, breaking into primetime television with announcements to parents to take their children out of the room. The fear that war could break out at any moment hung heavily, but the eerie silence of unspoken words made it feel worse.

I believe overcompensation, particularly by the entertainment world's use of boundless optimism to distract us from the darker realities of the Cold War, contributed in no small way to the unwavering idealism of many in my generation including myself.

On special occasions we went to work with our father. This was always very exciting and fun. He did not take us all at once, usually one or two at a time. I loved going with him; it was always fun even though we had to be well behaved for long periods while he worked and absolutely quiet while scenes were shot. Once, when everyone was milling around and talking among themselves, I noticed the large director's chair facing one of the nearby sets was empty. I had never seen one so tall, all dark leather. I was fascinated, so I sneaked over, climbed up onto it, and settled in. Suddenly there was laughter, and a huge handsome man leaned over me and said, "Hey, partner, that's my chair." It was rugged movie icon John Wayne, and I instantly was smitten. He playfully helped me down. For the first time, I had real awareness of a man from the viewpoint of a woman. They really were very different! No wonder the women in the movies made such a fuss over them.

The movie sets were filled mostly with men. I loved it when men got together, and I loved the humor that took place. I laughed out loud and so hard. My father picked up on this and amusedly encouraged me to chime in. I happily obliged, making them laugh all the harder. Barbara often picked us up from the set. When she saw me laughing loudly and boldly contributing to the jokes and conversations, she disapproved, calling my behavior "common"— not how girls my age should behave, she said. When I persisted, she took the matter to my mother, who went directly to my father and told him not to encourage me. It wasn't good for me, my mother urged. I was already too frank for my own good, she pointed out.

She was right. Even though I loved making my father and his friends laugh, I really didn't understand why they were laughing. I was just telling them what I thought. When they asked my opinion on Bob's new haircut, I replied that it was better I didn't say anything because I had nothing nice to say. Or if they asked me why I liked Fred, I told them he reminded me of a turtle with his round body and bald head bobbing at the top. As to how I felt about Edith, my father's secretary, well, she always made me feel welcome and happy—she reminded me of an overweight Hawaiian Howdy Doody.

In third grade, I was suspended from school and almost expelled for saying what I thought was the right thing. Even my father, my greatest ally, was chastened by this incident. My mother blamed him, saying it never would have happened if he hadn't emboldened me. My teacher became ill for several weeks, and we were given a substitute nun named Sister Marietta. Usually we were a very good class, but we became extremely unruly. After about a week, Sister Marietta was desperate, even hysterical, praying to us with folded hands that we be good and quiet. But of course, we only acted worse. Looking back, I suppose we sensed her weakness and just couldn't resist since it was too easy.

Finally one day, tears in her eyes, Sister Marietta begged us to tell her why we behaved so badly. Perhaps it was a rhetorical question, but I thought she wanted an answer. I looked around. No one dared to raise a hand. So I bravely raised mine, thinking the rest of the class cowardly for not letting her know. She called on me, and I said, "Sister, we wouldn't laugh so hard if you shaved your mustache."

Sister Marietta screamed at me and cried, "You evil child! Get out of this class." I was escorted immediately to the principal's office. I was shocked by the reaction. I had genuinely thought she might be grateful for my candid assessment. My mother and Barbara came to the school to pick me up. They spent a long time with the principal. When they finally came out, neither spoke to me at first.

Barbara finally said quietly, "It took all we could to keep you from getting expelled. If your mother were not who she is, you would have been thrown out." I was suspended from school and grounded at home for two weeks. I wasn't allowed to play outside. I cried hard at that thought. That night, my mother came to my room and asked if I understood the gravity of what I'd said. She told me I had gone too far with my needlessly cruel remarks. I tried to convince her I didn't know I was doing anything wrong. I thought I was doing the right thing by telling the truth. Sister Marietta had asked us to tell her. My mother said I needed time to think about what I had done. She hoped I would learn a lesson from this and understand it is not funny to hurt people's feelings. I was a thoughtless girl, she continued, and it was time for me to grow up and get over this frankness and realize it is not cute. Hurting people has consequences, she emphasized before leaving the room. I tried very hard to think of how I had done the wrong thing, but I just didn't get it.

Mia also tried very diligently to help me grasp this, but eventually even she gave up. She concluded by telling me the story of a school friend's grandfather who had been very unhappy for a long time. Finally, doctors decided they had to take drastic measures and gave him what I later learned was called a lobotomy. They went through his nose and surgically snipped the attachment between the two sides of his brain. Since then he says and does things that hurt people's feelings all the time, Mia explained. We both remembered that I had fallen very hard on my head the first time I climbed onto the Bed of the Big Tree. The fall must have caused a part of the connection between the two sides of my brain to tear. We agreed that this was probably the reason I didn't understand I had done anything wrong and likely would never understand. I felt saddened by this, but at least I now knew why. When I tried to relay all this to Barbara, exasperated she angrily hissed, "Don't you *dare* try and give that excuse to your mother!"

Even though all this occurred several weeks before Thanksgiving, it cast a cloud over my Christmas holiday. Its entire buildup, which was usually so exciting and full of joy, was overshadowed by my certainty that my stocking would be packed with coal. I envied my friends' innocence as they talked of writing letters to Santa Claus, decorating fir trees, and general holiday excitement. For me, it was the opposite. Each holiday ritual was more painful than the next as I dreaded each day Christmas drew near.

By the time Christmas morning arrived, I was a wreck. Neither Barbara nor my mother could imagine what was wrong with me. If only I could have told them, but I was too ashamed. I stoically faced the inevitable, reluctantly entering the living room and moving toward the fireplace where our stockings hung. Mine was bulging. I thought to myself how mean it was of the elves to go out of their way to stuff it so full that it looked laden with presents. I watched Mia and the other children pull their toys out, and I almost cried. Reaching for my stocking, I saw peeking out of the top a little cloth monkey's head with a red hat. I had toys!

Besides the toys that were purchased for us, my older brothers were notorious in our neighborhood for building rowdy things. They made their own go-karts, racing them up and down the alleyways in the afternoons until late in the evening. We had a gravel backyard with a huge walnut tree in the center. My brothers dug a deep moat around the tree's trunk, filled it with water, and built a large fort high up in the tree. The rest of the graveled area was scattered with an array of tiny military tanks and vehicles and lead soldiers spread around in a cratered, beat-up range filled with bombed-out holes from war games. We often heard small bombs going off as part of their war experiments. They carried BB guns everywhere and sometimes shot at anyone on the sidewalks near the house, finding it especially hilarious when they hit people and heard them scream. They took shots at all the animals in the area, often killing squirrels. One Christmas, they stayed up all night ready to shoot and capture Santa when he delivered presents.

My father had the boys take boxing lessons to divert some of their energy. My oldest brother, Michael, was the nicest; Patrick, the middle one, was meanest. When the ice-cream man came with his musical van, Patrick and his friends took the cones right out of our hands and laughed as they walked away, licking them. One summer day I was drinking a ginger ale and playing in front of the Roach house when Patrick walked right up to me, said it was a very hot day, and snatched my drink from my hand. I screamed, "Give it back to me! It's *mine.*"

Patrick turned, laughing. "Now it's mine." I was so angry I could only sob. One of his friends, finding compassion for me, grabbed it and handed it back.

FAMILY POSES FOR COLD WAR
ADVERTISEMENT: JOHN, PATRICK,
PRUDENCE, MAUREEN, STEFFI,
MIA, MICHAEL AND JOHNNY 1952

MariaRoachbirthdaypartyat
the Roach Home 1952

Mia and Johnny directing
Prudence for home movie
1952

Roach swimming pool,
bathhousesandtenniscourt

Prudenceage6yearsold1954

seven

A World Upside Down

It was the winter of 1957 to '58. I was just nine years old, soon to be ten, when our world was upended. Life had been going along quite happily, and there was no reason to believe it would not continue. But that was not the way things were to be. The foreboding winds of change soon took most everything we held dear.

The holiday season was always a particularly happy time. We christened the start of another Christmas, as usual, with our annual Thanksgiving feast, as the whole family gathered in our parents' dining room to eat. My mother had decorated the house with holiday lights, and the dining table was brightly lit by four large silver candelabras. Christmas music was playing in the background, and everyone was cheerful.

The table was so richly adorned with food that its white, smartly pressed tablecloth of Irish linen and lace was barely visible beneath the multicolored china bowls filled with bright-orange freshly cut sweet potatoes, deep-green collards, vividly green peas, crimson cranberries, dark-brown mushroom gravy, snap beans speckled with sliced almonds, yellow squash, glistening sliced tomatoes, deliciously buttered mashed potatoes, and wild rice. At the center of this feast was an enormous, beautifully basted, and perfectly cooked stuffed turkey set between the candelabras. We would eat this for days afterward. The side table along the wall was covered in pumpkin pies, apple strudel, freshly whipped cream, cut strawberries, and chocolate soufflé. The candlelit room shimmered warmly across the bright silver serving bowls and glimmering silverware placed neatly on the table.

After our prayer of gratitude, we were allowed to pull, snap, and tear open our colorful party poppers, placed beside each of our dinner plates. Inside were party hats, whistles, tiny toys, fortunes, and jokes. We had a lot of fun as the room filled with noisy whistles, horns, popping sounds, and laughter as we read our jokes out loud. The house could barely contain the mirth projected by all of us. Finally, the evening ended with our singing Christmas carols. My mother and father both seemed so happy.

Just after Thanksgiving, my mother brought out our nativity sets from the large storage room closet. We all had our own sets, each slightly different from the other. We delicately unpacked them from their wooden boxes, unwrapping pieces from their tissue-paper covering and carefully setting them up on bedside bureaus. Each set consisted of individually hand-carved wooden pieces. Mine had twelve pieces: two sheep (one lying down), one donkey (also lying down), two shepherds, three wise men, Mary, Joseph, baby Jesus, and his little crib with straw carved into the wood. All the pieces were placed in a little open barn with a tiny light at the top. I loved the light, which stayed lit day and night throughout the Christmas season.

We each also received an advent calendar to start on the first of December. There was a tiny toy in each shuttered window, to be opened every day of the month leading up to Christmas Day. But my favorite part of the calendar was the little wise saying hidden behind each toy. They were simple sayings such as "A stitch in time saves nine" or "A bird in hand is worth two in the bush."

A few joyful days after Thanksgiving, our mother arranged for our cook Marcel's older daughter Betty to babysit us. She was nineteen and tons of fun—we laughed with her for hours. She took us girls to the movie theater to see *Gone with the Wind*, and we cried our hearts out. For weeks after, I was accused of emulating Scarlett O'Hara's behavior (it was true) and had no sense of humor when my sisters pointed this out to me.

Every Christmas, the neighborhood children formed small committees headed by the older children for the purpose of making decorations, like colorful candles. Mia's committee always made the best decorations. We embellished everything in sight, decking out my mother's bedroom with garlands of fir branches over the doors and strings of lights around her nativity set. We made a huge picture of a Christmas tree, covered in sequins and adorned with elves and angels, and put it on the front door. We scattered small pictures of cutout stars and trees across our bathroom mirrors. Marcel helped us cut and make cookies. For several years, we went to neighborhood houses singing carols. One year, Mia headed a small nativity play.

The night for decorating the tree finally arrived. We lined up impatiently at the entrance to the living room waiting for our parents' call to enter, like racehorses waiting in their stalls before the start of a race. Our living room was large and rectangular with two huge wooden doors and hallways leading into it. We usually entered from the end that led into our bedrooms. The door at the other end led to our parents' dining room and their kitchen. One side of the room was filled with spacious windows and a sliding glass door that opened onto the central patio. On the other side of the room were two bay windows with cushioned seats, looking out onto the front garden. A large stone fireplace with a roaring, crackling fire occupied the wall between them. The fireplace was warmly decorated with bright, colorful Christmas lights and an enormous fir wreath with a big, red bow in the center. Seven hooks were distributed along the stone mantel above the fireplace for us to hang our stockings.

At last Barbara opened the door and told us our parents were ready for us to trim the tree. Standing like a sentry at the door, Barbara warned us in a loud voice not to run. Of course we had already burst past her through the door and were racing toward the tree. Decorating the Christmas tree was the culmination of a grand finale for all our decorating efforts, as our parents watched all the children participate in hanging hand-painted ornaments; lights with yellow, green, or red liquid bubbling up; and bulbs of all shapes, colors, and sizes. The tree was situated at the far end of the room in front of the window.

It was already surrounded at its base by many colorfully wrapped presents. Upon seeing two or three enormous wrapped boxes, we could barely contain ourselves. This year my brother Michael was old enough to climb the small ladder and place at the top of the tree a porcelain angel dressed in a white-velvet gown with attached sequined wings. The finishing touch was throwing and draping thin strips of glistening metallic-icicle tinsel over the pine needles.

Finally we all got cups of hot chocolate with marshmallows while my mother handed out our handwoven Christmas stockings. Each of us had our names woven in our own stocking with individual patterns of Christmas trees, angels, stars, poinsettias, elves, or Santa. Mine was deep red with the scene of a little house surrounded by bright flowers and several happy elves dressed in green. One by one, we each ceremoniously placed a stocking on its hook. Tisa, who was six, still needed help putting hers up. By the time this was done, Christmas madness was in full swing.

The mirth and joy of Thanksgiving had officially shifted into the frenzied craziness of Christmastime, only this year we children were wilder than ever before, swinging tempestuously between bouts of uncontrollable excitement and fits of emotional hysteria. I don't know if any of us realized it at the time, but now it's clear that our cantankerous behavior came about because we had been told we would be leaving our home after the holidays.

Our mother brought us younger children into her room one evening shortly after Thanksgiving, explaining she had a very special surprise to tell us. Freshly bathed, our hair brushed one hundred strokes by Barbara, and in clean nightgowns, robes, and slippers, we gathered around our mother. In her lovely lyrical voice, she began a tale about a little hand-carved boat a little boy set downstream on a long winding journey. We were enthralled. Then she told us our father would be making another long journey. He was working on another big movie and would be traveling far away. Only this time, he didn't want to leave us—he wanted to take us with him. "Would you like to go on a journey?" She asked. "Yes!" we shouted back excitedly.

Our mother had cleverly addressed the whole event with the glass-is-half-full approach. Every night it seemed, she read us stories about children who lived far away. I remember reading about the little boy who lived in New York City and lost his way home from school. He was picked up by a policeman and rode all the way home through the streets of the city on the back of a horse. I was entranced for I had only known policemen on motorcycles. Another little boy in England wore knee-high socks and rode to school through London in a red double-decker bus. It was amazing and fascinating to me that there were such things as double-decker buses and socks up to your knees.

My mother's tactics worked very well. She bought us each a beautiful set of new luggage. My suitcases were made of a green-plaid cloth, and Mia's and Steffi's were red plaid. Tisa's plaid was a dark blue. Mia didn't seem to care much for hers, but Steffi and I loved ours. All the girls were given matching blue-tweed wool coats with velvet collars. I had never had a wool coat. All this was so exciting. I enjoyed packing my new winter clothes: beautiful sweaters, lovely pressed-cotton shirts and dresses, wool underwear, flannel nightgowns, heavy robes, and fuzzy slippers. I was even given my own pair of knee-high socks! The lack of plaid-flannel shirts, blue jeans, and PF Flyers was a little disturbing but quickly forgotten in the excitement of the moment.

My father was hired to direct a mega film on the life of the "Father of the US Navy," John Paul Jones. The film, aptly titled *John Paul Jones,* required extravagant expenditures with fabulous costly sets and costumes and an inordinate amount of extras. The producer was Samuel Bronston, known for producing this and other epic films such as *King of Kings* (1961), *El Cid* (1961), *55 Days at Peking* (1963), and *The Fall of the Roman Empire* (1964). In 1962, he was awarded a Special Merit Golden Globe Award for *El Cid*.

Many people in the movie business make large amounts of money in a very short time. According to what I gathered from overheard conversations between my parents, whenever a person made a large lump sum of money, the income taxes were very high. I was pretty sure I heard my father say the government would take 80 percent of the money. To keep a large portion of the money from being taxed, he had to live abroad for two years. He decided to do the postproduction work in England and lease out our home while we were gone. But after about a month, my parents made the rash decision to sell our house and its entire furnishings. My mother regretted this in the years ahead. I think with all the confusion and problems of trying to store our belongings, move, and find renters, they became overwhelmed and made a last-minute choice to just sell everything.

The house was sold dirt-cheap to practically the first interested buyer. It seemed as if at this point my parents just wanted to get out of town fast. Many family valuables and heirlooms were lost in the flurry to quick storage. There was no foresight. It felt as if everything was thrown to the wind. From a child's perspective, it all moved too rapidly. I was living in a constant state of disbelief. I just watched, as Barbara and my mother boxed up many of my favorite toys and treasured belongings. My mother tried to soften the blow of leaving everything we loved behind, promising that none of our valuables would be given away but kept in storage for when we returned. She engaged us by having us help with the packing.

At this point, I suddenly became unhinged. While boxing up my most beloved stuffed animals for their long confinement, I had the realization that all this upheaval and moving was madness. Someone had to stop it, and if no one would, *I* would! "We can't do this!" I shouted to Barbara and my mother at the top of my lungs. "None of it makes any sense. I refuse to go along with it!" I screamed.

The more vocal I grew, the more adamant I became. Ripping open the box I had just packed, I grabbed my dearest animals. "I won't let it happen!" I cried. My mother reached for me, but I had already started for the door. Barbara grabbed my leg, and I frantically hit her. "You don't know what you are doing. Why should I listen to any of you?" I yelled. I wanted to run as far away as possible. They were all crazy. Tearing myself loose from Barbara's grip, while clutching my dearly beloved bears close to my chest, I raced down the hall toward the front door.

My mother and Barbara quickly followed. I felt I was running for my life, even though I didn't know where. Michael tackled me in the front yard. I hated him. Even though I was kicking, screaming, shouting, hitting, biting, and scratching, they all somehow managed to pin me down. I wanted to die. "I hate you. I hate you," I cried over and over again. It was all I could say. As my mother held me firmly, she kept repeating, "Calm down, calm down." The whole Roach family came out to see the commotion. But it wasn't until I saw the perplexed face of my youngest sister, Tisa, six at the time, looking at me from behind Barbara, that I suddenly sobered. Then all I could do was cry. For the first time since hearing we were leaving, I sobbed my heart out.

That night my mother had me climb into bed with her. She did this sometimes with each of us. We hugged each other tightly, while she gently stroked my hair just as she had when I was very young. When I awoke the next morning, an adorable new pink smiling bear lay beside me. He was in his underwear. Near his paw was a little suitcase filled with two shirts, a pair of shorts, a pair of long pants, and a little nightshirt and cap. My mother had bought him for me. I loved him instantly and knew he would fill the vacuum left by moving. I named him Pinky.

During Christmas vacation, my mother had afternoon tea with me and sometimes Steffi, too. Once school was back in session, she picked Steffi and me up after school, bringing us back to her kitchen where Eileen, our parents' cook, had tea brewing with wonderful pink-and-white-flowered cookies served on the best china. I loved our afternoon teas. When my cup was empty, my mother read my tea leaves, looking at how the leaves were arranged, and told me what she saw ahead were wonderful happy times to come.

I then tried to read her leaves, and she told me how wise I was, just like Prudence should be.

After a week back in school, she began picking us up early and taking us home, where Eileen prepared us sandwiches and soup. During this period, into mid-January, I looked forward to the daily afternoon visits with my mother. Sometimes, she asked us lots of questions. I was surprised when she told me she never understood all the new gadgets our father and Eileen continuously brought into the kitchen. She told Steffi and me to look over the stove in her kitchen at the big hole chipped out of the ceiling. This was from the new pressure cooker our father brought her just before Thanksgiving. It blew up the first time she used it. She said she would never understand how it worked.

One special evening right after I had received Pinky, my mother called me into her room before bedtime. She told me we would pray together tonight for God to watch over us and make us strong on the long journey ahead. Before we knelt to pray, she asked, "You remember the story I told you about the Gypsy?"

I responded with a hearty "yes!" for we all loved to hear her tell us about her meeting with the Gypsy, making her repeat it to us endlessly over the years. "I told you the Gypsy predicted my future life here in America. But the important thing is not what she told me but what she showed me. Life is magical. You must never forget that. It is full of mystery and unknowns that sometimes frighten us. But you must not be afraid. In your heart you are always safe. Remember life is made up of what is seen and what is not seen. Few people bother with what they don't see. You must pay attention to the unseen, however, for what is not seen holds the key to all that you see. In the unseen, things don't always make sense. They follow different rules. For instance, in the unseen, we are all connected together in one Spirit with nothing ever to fear. How can that be? The Spirit knows no separation or loss. These belong to the realm of what is seen."

It was clear she deeply and sincerely wanted me to understand what she was saying. Even though I hadn't understood a word of it, I knew from her fervent demeanor that it was important. By the time we finished our prayers, I had a sense of what she was trying to tell me. As we prayed, a quiet soft embracing silence enveloped us. I felt a tremendous peace and wanted us to stay like this forever. I looked at my mother's beatific face, which appeared almost translucent, and she smiled ever so softly. I hung on to this moment, knowing I would remember it the rest of my life.

After the house was put up for sale, we continued living in it until we moved. It had become almost completely emptied of all but the barest necessities. It was very eerie living there, a poignant metaphor and reminder of the finality of a significant period of our lives. Mia described it as the end of her childhood. For me, it was closure to the happiest and most stable time of my life. But as much as the emptiness symbolized an ending, it was also an omen to the beginning of an era of relentless upheaval, a harbinger of perceived loss and tumult yet to come. Living those last weeks in the backdrop of our empty home was like being on a movie set that had once been full and vibrant with life and was now devoid of all paraphernalia, props, and role players. It was a "wrap."

eight

Upheaval: Travels in Spain

I clearly remember the morning we left. It was early February 1958. I had just turned ten, having celebrated my birthday at the end of January. Our excited anticipation knew no bounds. We were going on our first plane ride, an eight-hour propeller flight from Los Angeles to New York City. My father and Barbara traveled cross-country with us children, while my mother went on ahead to set up the necessary arrangements. In those days, we had to go outside onto the airport's tarmac to enter the plane. The roar of the propeller planes was almost deafening. We had to scream at one another to be heard. Michael grabbed my hand as I was suddenly lifted into the air by the blast from the propellers.

Once onboard, I got to sit next to my father, because, I think, the older children were old enough to sit by themselves, while Barbara had her hands full with the two youngest. At ten years old, I still needed to be looked after. I couldn't believe my good fortune in being the one child who got to sit next to my father. I knew the other children, especially Mia and Johnny, were very aware of this. All the while, I could feel their eyes on me as I hugged his arm tightly, guiltily gloating over my fortuity.

The takeoff was a letdown after the excitement of boarding the plane, with the thundering noise of the engines and blast of the propellers. Overall, the flight was mostly uneventful. We landed at Idlewild Airport, now known as John F. Kennedy International Airport, and then we drove into New York City. It was a long drive to the city, and there were stretches of barren land with sparsely distributed homes.

It was the first time I'd experienced snow. I watched, enthralled, from the limousine window, seeing other children my age playing in the snow, ice skating on frozen ponds, and sledding on small hills that looked steeper than they probably were. They seemed like storybook children. These scenes stuck in my mind more than the huge tall buildings of Manhattan and its congested streets crammed with honking traffic and crowds of pedestrians packing the sidewalks and spilling into the roads. I saw people swearing and shouting at each other for the first time. The reason it was not more shocking was that the picture books my mother showed us prepared me perhaps too well for the crowded streets of Manhattan with its chaos and congestion.

What lingers in my mind was Central Park, beautiful countryside placed contrarily in the middle of the fray of the big city. We stayed only two days in Manhattan before leaving for Spain. Barbara took the younger children—Johnny, Steffi, Tisa, and me—to ride through the park in a horse-drawn carriage. When we stopped for a moment in front of the ice-skating rink, we begged to be let out of the carriage to build a snowman in the white-blanketed field nearby and to ice-skate in the outdoor rink. Barbara was adamant, arguing that we were not dressed properly for the snow. Further pleading from us finally broke her down. Excitedly removing the woolen blankets that covered our legs, we piled out of the warm comfortable environment of the carriage. Much to our surprise and dismay, she was right. We never imagined that the miraculous fluffy white snow we had seen in movies and books was freezing cold!

We stayed on Fifth Avenue, just five blocks from Central Park, at the elegantly luxurious eighteen-story St. Regis Hotel, built in the early 1900s in French Beaux-Arts style. Many famous people had permanent apartments there over the years, including actress Marlene Dietrich and artist Salvador Dali. Everything inside appeared to be trimmed with gold inlay.

Having arrived in New York on a Friday, its main attractions were full of other weekend tourists. We visited the Empire State Building, waiting in long lines, shuffling interminably in packed crowds through hallways and up and down stairwells. I was short enough to feel endlessly confined to the area below people's shoulders. When I finally had a view of the startling heights, it was amazing but way too brief as we were hurriedly rushed along to allow room for the many tourists that followed us.

I was sad to leave the city. Its vitality with so many people, each living with such palpitating purpose, was exhilarating. I watched once again from the window of the limousine, the same scenes I saw when we arrived, scenes of lone houses with children ice-skating on small frozen ponds and playing in the snow. Only this time, I felt a level of melancholy as I reflected on the individual lives I would never know deeply but now cared about in some way. These were not picture-book people anymore but people I'd gotten to know, however briefly.

Late on a Monday afternoon, we boarded another propeller airplane for Spain, a Pan Am flight flying from Idlewild Airport into Madrid. The flight took sixteen hours, with a brief stopover in Lisbon. We were very excited, but even more than the adventure of the flight and traveling to far-off Spain was the prospect of spending so many hours in close proximity to our father. We so missed seeing him and knew our chances of being with him later would be rare, especially now that he was directing a mega film.

Mia and I had already heatedly worked out between us who got to sit with our father first during this flight. Of course, she would spend the first half of the flight in the seat next to him. We didn't take into account that the plane had sleepers, and that by 9:00 p.m. eastern time, we would climb into our individual curtained bunk beds for an eight-hour snooze. Mia was on the bottom bunk, and I slept on the top. During the night, the plane hit heavy turbulence that caused it to drop dramatically. I was in a pleasant state of semi-consciousness, enjoying sensations in my stomach caused by the diving plane, much like a ride on a roller coaster, when suddenly my father and Barbara ripped open the curtains and dragged Mia, me, and the other children from our beds and into our seats.

We were in the midst of a raging storm. Lightning flashed continually between violent bouts of the plane's plunging. After several sudden and particularly pitched plane dives, everyone on board was screaming. I sat next to my father, clutching his arm and looking up into his face. Just being close to him, even in a situation like this, was such a thrill. I heard poor Barbara and the other children scream. As my father repeatedly turned around in his seat to check on them, I remained blissfully oblivious to the potential danger. I just watched my father, his strong, sensitive face. I had vague thoughts about missing confession, mortal sin, and hell, but these merely rambled impotently in the back of my mind. I was with my father and, somehow, I was safe, so even such frightening thoughts couldn't disturb me.

We eventually made an emergency landing in the Azores, west of Portugal, amid torrential rain, flashing lightning, and heavy winds. As we began our rocky descent toward the group of volcanic islands, I suddenly felt a piercing agonizing pain in my ears. My poor father was beside himself, what with the perilous descent, my hysteria over my ears, and his futile attempts at trying to calm the other children. We finally arrived at the airport in Madrid nearly twenty-four hours after we had left New York. My first memory of Spain was the smell. It was so different, the smell of a foreign land.

I was taken aback when first exposed to the friendliness and warmth of the Spanish children. My parents had friends, and friends of friends, who were Spanish. Many of these friends were the rich-and-famous, such as controversial Spanish dictator Francisco Franco and his family, along with his extended network of friends and their children. Of course I had no idea at the time that Franco was part of a military coup, which overthrew the democratic republic government and started the Spanish Civil War (1936-1939). A half million lives were lost in that war, which Franco eventually won and then set up a totalitarian state that lasted until his death in 1975.

Shortly after we arrived, my parents arranged for us to visit these families, who took us to playgrounds, boating in Buen Retiro Park, exploring the lavish Royal Palace of Madrid, and to birthday parties. The children always welcomed us by pinching our cheeks and calling out, "*que guapa*" ("how pretty"). I was often much taller than my Spanish counterparts who, undeterred, warmly took my hand to lead me around. It didn't matter whether or not the children knew us—everyone made friends with us.

We stayed at the Castellano Hilton Hotel. Although my parents were around sometimes, my father worked most of the time while my mother was busy with social duties, which included meeting and partying with the necessary politicians and wealthy Spanish patrons of the film and their wives. Michael came with us to Spain to help our parents with the move, but soon after we arrived, he went back to the United States, to our nation's capital, to attend Georgetown University. Patrick, Johnny, and Mia periodically worked on set as actors in minor parts. Johnny played a twelve-year-old John Paul Jones, Patrick had the role of a young sailor, and Mia had a small uncredited part.

We girls were enrolled in an elite Spanish private day school that Franco's daughter Marta attended. During our free time, Barbara was busy with Tisa and Steffi, so the rest of us, Mia, Johnny, and I, were often left on our own. We quickly befriended the only other American child, a nine-year-old girl called Lizzy, whose father was the hotel manager.

The hotel, massive in size, had a labyrinth of shops, eating areas, ice cream and soda fountains, beauty parlors, offices, convention rooms, ballrooms, and bars. The first thing Lizzy introduced us to was a delicious chocolate milkshake served at one of the local ice cream shops. Lizzy was a little overweight from constant indulgence in the candies, cakes, and ice cream continuously offered to her whenever she passed by a store. Perhaps this was because of the position her father held, or it might have been due to the warm and friendly nature of the Spanish people, who seemed to adore children.

The elevator boys were another source of amusement. They teased and played tricks on us. But most memorable was exploring the massive hotel complex. After about a month, Lizzy took us aside, whispering very low while looking furtively over her shoulder, "You three are finally ready to visit the hidden room." Looking carefully from side to side, she continued in a hoarse whisper, "I've waited until I was sure you could be trusted. You must promise never to reveal to anyone what I am about to tell you." Mia was suspicious and wanted no part of it. To my surprise, Lizzy instantly dropped the subject. I was intensely intrigued, and Lizzy knew it.

Shrewdly biding her time, Lizzy waited patiently until Mia and Johnny had left. "I know you want to go to the hidden room," she said. "If I take you, you must swear on your life as my blood sister that you shall not tell anyone about this." The week before, in one of the hotel's dark stairwells, she and I had secretly sworn loyalty as blood sisters by poking our fingers with the tip of her father's razor and putting our bloodied wounds together. Lizzy went on to describe what she called a "gangsters' club." I became terrified—what if we were caught? She assured me with utter confidence that she had been there many times and no one had caught her. Looking around carefully to be sure no one was in earshot, she whispered, "We will go tomorrow night." Her absolute confidence, mixed with an almost tangible sense of danger, made her offer irresistible to me. I solemnly swore my allegiance.

We decided I would slip out after Barbara had seen that I had gone to bed and was firmly asleep. By the next evening, I was very frightened and wanted out of the whole thing. But I had given my word and felt there was no way out. I hated that I could not tell Mia or Steffi, but they would only get angry and prevent me from going. Being out late at night was no problem for Lizzy. Her parents were much more lenient than mine. She was used to prowling around the hotel well after our bedtime, which was now 8:30 p.m. Her family had grown accustomed to the Spanish culture with its daily one o'clock siesta time and late dinner around ten. Lizzy and I decided to meet in front of the barbershop at 9:00 p.m. Luckily, Steffi, who slept in the other bed next to mine, went right to sleep this night.

When meeting, I once again was made to solemnly swear on my honor never to go looking for this room on my own. We hastily raced toward the nearest stairway upon which, to my surprise, I was made to stand still while blindfolded with a thin scarf. Lizzy led me stealthily down more stairs and through what seemed to be narrow winding corridors and metal stairways. At last, we came to a small bookcase. Lizzy removed the thin scarf and pulled back on the bookcase, which opened like a door into a large dark room. We had to climb down several stairs to enter. I could faintly see a small stage at the far end of the room.

Lizzy pulled a large switch behind us. There was a loud pop, and two huge bright dangling chandeliers suddenly lit up the room. Many little tables and chairs were placed haphazardly throughout. A little stage was slightly elevated on a wooden platform. Nearby was a drum set, a clarinet, and several brass instruments. Used cigarette and cigar butts were strewn around. The place was messy. It obviously had been used recently.

Lizzy, grabbing a cigar and putting it suavely between her lips, pretended to smoke while I played the drums. She danced. Knowing we were in a forbidden and dangerous place put us in a state of euphoria. We helped ourselves to handfuls of different nuts from the abundant supply of small bowls placed on the tables and along a sideboard. We ate nuts until our stomachs were bursting and we could eat no more. Lizzy looked madly behind the long heavy red drapery, which hung full-length from ceiling to floor, for packages of gum in the small drawers that lined the walls. We sat at different tables, posing as gangsters, and danced drunkenly together as we imagined they would.

Finally it was time to go. Glowing from our adventure, we raced back to our rooms through a maze of hallways, corridors, and stairwells. I somehow managed to sneak back into my bedroom and bed unnoticed. Proud of my newly acquired deceptive abilities, I contentedly slipped into a self-satisfied sleep. But later that night, severe and unbearable pains in my stomach abruptly broke my slumber. Sweating and feverish, I yelled out for help. All I remember is a frantic collage of flickering shadows, voices, and lights, interrupted only by my crying, screaming, and moaning.

Hoping to rid myself of my suffering, which I saw as direct retribution for the evening's debauchery and deception, between yelps, I incoherently tried to confess my sins but to no avail. When I yelled out words like "gangsters' club" or "drum set," no one knew what I was saying. But when I finally said the words "endless bowls of nuts," the doctor, having arrived a few minutes earlier, instantly determined this unlimited nut supply must have exacerbated what appeared to be an acute case of appendicitis. I was immediately rushed by ambulance to the hospital, where my appendix was promptly removed. No one, not even Mia, suspected my misdeeds. I guiltily enjoyed everyone's sympathy. Eventually I told them, but by that point no one even wanted to hear.

The morning after my operation, I awoke in an ethereal stupor and saw my mother standing at my bedside while Barbara lingered in the doorway. I reached over to hug my mother and wailed from the unanticipated pain. As I cried desperately, the pain increased with the pressure from each sob. My mother leaned over, hugging me gently and telling me softly not to move anymore. It will be all right soon, she promised. I fell fast asleep. Upon finally awakening, I saw my mother and Barbara slumped over in the two chairs opposite the bed. They were obviously exhausted. I wanted to yell out to them that I was awake and hug them, but I didn't dare move or speak for fear of the pain.

Much to my delight, my mother was there to take me home from the hospital and had pulled Barbara from her duties with the younger children. Barbara was devotedly attentive to me, staying with me in my hospital room during my weeklong stay and continuing to dote on me well after I returned to the hotel.

nine

Upheaval: Adventures in Spain

A month or so later, we traveled with Barbara to the coastal town of Benidorm, along the Mediterranean shore, a hot spot for German tourists. My mother had rented a small bungalow for the summer. We traveled from one chateau to another with a chauffeur hired by our father. The journey took several days. We took turns riding with our mother, who followed behind us in the new red-and-black Karmann Ghia our father had just bought for her. The whole way, Mia and I fought over who got to have which room and which younger sister as a roommate.

Our driver, Vicente, arrived in a baby-blue Cadillac. We took our time, sightseeing along the way, stopping at the ruins of castles and old churches. We drove through fascinating villages buried in cliffs, alongside rivers, with narrow winding cobblestone streets and small stone bridges with rushing water below. We passed through one such village that was located along a sewage outlet. The smell was atrocious. But the people were used to it, looking and acting normally as any other people from any other village. As we passed along the road and over the small bridge above the large sewer,

I saw a girl about my age. She was barefoot, in a long dirty dress, walking with her family. Trailing casually behind her was a small donkey piled high with cloth-covered packages. Looking out my window, I stared hard at her and thought, *I shall never forget your face.*

We stayed overnight in little chateaus or hotels. They were, for the most part, grungy and dirty. I felt depressed by them. The mattresses were unusually sunken and sagging. Barbara found a nest of bedbugs in one. I did love the apricot marmalade we predictably had in the mornings wherever we stayed, but I didn't like the orange. Mia and Johnny were the opposite.

I also felt discouraged at the thought of sleeping in so many strange beds. Barbara always carried her own pillow with her when she traveled. When she was young, she traveled with her family from Scotland to Italy, staying in many different places. She said she always felt profoundly sad upon leaving the different beds, knowing others shared love and deep thoughts in the same pillows and bedding.

We finally arrived in Benidorm. Barbara stayed with us the first two weeks, but then she traveled to Scotland to visit her family for several weeks. My father hired a young Swedish woman, Margareta, to take care of us during this time. Margareta spoke fluent English and Spanish. The little bungalow house we lived in was at the end of a dirt street, about a block and a half from the sea. It was made of mud stucco, painted white. Our father stayed in a large hotel in the center of Benidorm; Patrick and Johnny stayed with him. He came to see us sometimes but was mostly working in a little seaport called Denia. Our little house faced out onto a large hill, which had a big fancy lone hotel at the top. Our mother stayed in this hotel. Its entrance was at the end of a long winding road, the only paved road in the area.

At the end of our street was a desert-type area with small brush and little trees stretching as far as the eye could see. Our small hacienda had two bedrooms with large glassless windows decorated with thick cotton curtains. The air was always balmy and blew through the house, bringing in desert smells mixed with that of the sea. For some reason, we had a burro tied outside our back window. We never asked why but just accepted that it was there. We petted it often, and fed it grass and brush. Sometimes we untied it and walked it with us to the beach or in the desert. The burro made so much noise bleating at night that our father felt forced to get rid of it.

We had a Spanish cook and cleaning woman, young and stout Maria, who came every day. She laughed a lot and shook her hand like a fan in front of her face, repeating, "*que calor, que calor*"—"so hot." The only thing we were allowed to drink was wine, because everything else was too dangerous. There was no purification system for the water, and sanitation generally was not good, so drinking the water, even in a big sophisticated city like Madrid, was potentially hazardous. It was very common to pick up a microbe or amoeba. It was also considered unsafe to eat much of the meat because of worms, and drinking the milk, which was not homogenized, was deemed generally unsafe as well.

Maria made vats of sangria for us to drink. She gave us each our own little brightly painted glazed clay pot. In Spanish, with a splattering of a few basic English words like *cold, hot, no, yes, happy,* and *sad,* she explained that the pots were for keeping the sangria cold. We took the pots with us everywhere. Hand-painted on each pot was a beautiful pattern of flowers in vivid colors of red, green, and blue. Each pot had two open-raised spouts at the top. One was round for pouring the sangria in, and the other was spout-shaped for pouring into our mouths. Maria taught us to hold the pot above our heads and let the sangria pour through the air, never touching our lips, into our open waiting mouths. By the end of the summer, we got quite adept at it.

Every Sunday we attended mass in town, several miles away. The town was very small and dusty, spread out along a wide, unpaved road. There were lots of people about and many wooden-wheeled, donkey-drawn carts loaded high with goods. The shops were small, too, more like little vendors than storefronts. The church, at the end of the main street, seemed large compared to the diminution of everything else. In Catholicism in those days, all women were required to cover their heads in church. While in Madrid, we had bought several different-size lace veils, mantillas, for our heads.

I liked the long mantillas best but mostly wore short ones because they were simpler. The longer ones required more arranging so that they draped down the neck and fell at the shoulders properly. On my first visit to the church, the sight of a vast ocean of women wearing long black mantillas and fanning themselves fascinated me. They periodically opened and snapped shut their hand fans with the flick of their wrists. I had never seen anything like it. The fans were mostly large, very colorful and decorative, sometimes with feathers. The continuous snapping noise as the fans flicked open and then closed added to what seemed a very exotic scene.

Of course we girls all wanted our own fans. Barbara wasn't much interested in taking us shopping and kept putting it off to our great disappointment. But once Margareta came, we were able to indulge ourselves. She loved shopping and took us to town often. We walked up to the large street running along the water's edge at the end of our road, catching a ride into town on a burro cart. It wasn't always comfortable, but it was fun. In town was a store that sold knickknacks. We each combed carefully through the massive box of fans. I chose a hand-carved wooden fan with a design that looked almost like lace.

Mia chose a red silk fan with hand-painted flowers and lace trim. Steffi's looked almost Hawaiian. Margareta helped Tisa pick hers. It was probably the best of all of ours, made of silk with beautiful hand-painted birds. We loved our fans and spent hours mastering the art of snapping them open and shut with the flick of our wrists. We also spent one entire afternoon in the knickknack store, haggling over gold medallions to put on gold chains to be worn around our necks. I chose the Sacred Heart of Jesus. Mia chose Jesus with the crown of thorns.

One store in town was known to sell American hamburgers. We ate there regularly for a while until we heard it was horse meat we were eating and not beef. We also found out the wonderful delicate veal we were buying from the butcher was really cat meat. On

Saturday nights, the whole town gathered outside behind the church to watch an outdoor movie projected onto the church's large white wall. We watched several good movies, such as *Fantasia*, this way.

The beach was expansive. A substantial trek through the sandy landscape was required to reach the water from the road. As we neared the water, we saw beneath the sand remnants of old Roman stone roads extending deep into the waters. The Romans built roads from the beginning of their rule in 500 BC through its expansion and its fall. They were its arteries, carrying its armies and goods, built of stone to endure, networked throughout the empire. Along the beaches of Benidorm, some of these roads were still visible. Over time, the shifting of sea and sand covered them.

My father was particularly fascinated by these traces of history that marked the seascape. When he came to visit, our swimming took on new proportions, as he required us to swim out past the breakers. He had heard from the town's people and tourists that a shipwreck was buried several hundred feet past the breakers. My father thought diving to see this firsthand was an adventure we could not miss. The water was clear, so we could see the ship about twenty-five feet beneath us. He had us gradually dive deeper and deeper until our ears adjusted to the water pressure so that finally we would be able to reach the bottom. It was very frightening for me.

Soon the problem shifted from lessening the pressure in my ears to increasing the length of time I could hold my breath. I just couldn't reach down deep enough to touch the bottom where the ship was. But on the last day of our adventure with our father, I accomplished this under the hubris acquired when a bunch of other tourists were diving with us. Several slightly older boys egged Johnny and me on, taunting that we couldn't dive to the wreck. Under this influence, I made my most spectacular dive, going boldly and ever deeper until I touched the wreck at the bottom. Once there, I looked around madly for some souvenir to prove I had done it.

I frantically searched for anything. Finally grabbing at and tearing off a bit of barnacled wood, I looked up. Upon seeing the vast amount of water between me and the distant bright surface, my spirit almost collapsed. It was formidable. I had stayed too long and was already almost completely out of breath. Thoughts rushed all at once. *How will I make it that far? What have I done? Why hadn't I taken this into account? If only I hadn't spent so much time searching.* I swam desperately upward toward the surface. Halfway, my breath gave out. Forcing every ounce of strength and willpower I had, I clawed toward the surface. I couldn't make it. Terrified, I reached for the light but had nothing left to give and still a distance to go. My world was imploding—my strength was depleted. *It's over. I can't do it.*

Just then, my father, sensing my panic, swooped in and rushed me toward the surface. Coughing and gasping for some time, I finally asked him how he knew. He said he knew because he knew me. He had been watching me with the boys. When he saw my reaction to their taunting, that familiar look of determination in my eyes, he knew I would do whatever it took to prove myself. So when I didn't come up, he quickly took action. I swore in vain that I would never do anything like that again.

The next time my father came to visit, he took us on a boat ride to a little island not far off shore. We rode in a small beat-up boat, about the size of a rowboat, with a large loud oily smelly motor attached to its back. This island was known for the enormous stingrays and manta rays that circled it. Because of the clarity of the sea, we could see the dark flattened shapes of the many stingrays gliding silently and stealthily beneath and around us. Our father particularly loved the jellyfish-like man o' wars, whose opaque forms colored the sea. They appeared to be larger than our tiny rickety boat with their far-reaching tentacles stretching out below us. I imagined being enveloped by them after having been speared by the long rod-like tails of the stingrays, which could easily puncture our bow. I felt so vulnerable. None of us children enjoyed this part of our adventure in the least, but our father loved it. Our boat driver docked the small craft on the beach between the large rocks that shaped much of the island's shoreline.

Dark clouds moved in to cover the sun, and the sea, which had already been choppy, was growing rougher. Our driver warned that we must not stay long. We walked up and down large boulders, following our father for what seemed like forever as he gleefully pointed out small pools of tiny sea life captured in the bowels of the huge stones. All the while, the sea was churning up. Finally our father returned to the boat, which by this time was thrashing back and forth as the driver tried to commandeer it from being washed back out to sea. We jumped gingerly into the rocking boat.

The sea had become *very* rough. As we headed out, the swells had grown to five to ten feet high. Every time we went up and down one swell, another was looming above and appearing to crash upon us, but each time somehow we rode it out. Mia and Steffi became desperately sick. Steffi's face turned green, and she vomited incessantly the whole while. Later she said she was wishing she were dead. I prayed the whole time, certain we would die. It was cold, and the sea lashed us with a heavy spray as the bow of our little vessel broke through the top of the swells before pitching down again. After this, although we adored our father and loved to see him, we dreaded his future visits.

Toward the end of the summer, my father decided the younger children should visit the movie set. We didn't visit often, but it was always exciting to go on location. Mia, Johnny, and Patrick were already there since they had acting parts in the film. At that time, my father was filming battle scenes at sea, just off the seaport town of Denia. My memories of Denia are particularly vivid. My father used authentic sailing ships for the battle scenes. He commissioned Commander Alan Villiers, an Australian cousin of his, to put a fleet together. Alan had been a British naval officer in World War II and was well-known for having been the captain, just one year earlier, of the replica *Mayflower II* voyage across the Atlantic. He was an adviser on *John Paul Jones*, overseeing the refurbishment of two old sailing ships he had found in Sicily and the building of another ship in Barcelona to replicate the USS *Bonhomme Richard*.

Earlier in the summer in Benidorm, we had been on location while our father was filming battle scenes on land. He portioned off an enormous section of the beach and filled it with a population of thousands of Spanish extras as far as could be seen in every direction. Assistant director Emmet Emerson yelled, "Silence," and then the Spanish crew echoed, "*Silencio por favor*," all the way along what seemed like a good mile of men dressed as soldiers.

One day we were taken out on the replica of the three-masted, fully rigged frigate, *Bonhomme Richard*, which was carrying thirty to forty guns for a day of shooting in both senses of the word—shooting a movie *and* shooting weapons. The sea became particularly rough, with swells up to twenty feet. The ship was rising and dropping steeply. Facing yet another mountainous swell, we rose sharply again. It was amazing and I loved it, but the rest of my family, and practically everyone on board, became violently ill. For some reason my stomach loved that drop-like-a-roller-coaster feeling. My father, seeing I was genuinely thrilled, allowed me to be at the front of the ship as it dove way down and heaved sharply up. He arranged for one of the crew to hold me to the posts. It was a handsome young man my sister and I had crushes on—he had curly blond hair, and one gray eye and one green eye. He was color-blind.

One time in the port town of Denia, I ran into trouble just outside the set where the filming was taking place. The streets, lined by small shops, were crowded with curious spectators and filled with vendors selling goods. I was partially under the spell of an enormous infatuation with the film's photographer, named Hamm. He was an American in his thirties or older. My father said he was full of the devil, but everyone loved him. He was known for his passion for women and disappeared from time to time over some woman or other. That summer, he had brought with him to Spain a beautiful blond Swedish woman, who broke his heart. One day he gave me a camera, which was really a squirt gun. I wanted to get his attention, so I was showing off as he watched me playing in the street. I yelled, "Look, Hamm, I'm going to take some pictures."

He yelled back, "Be careful, Prudy." Delighted and emboldened by his attention, and not thinking at all what I was doing except that I might be amusing him, I headed boldly into the crowd with my camera. My parents and siblings were finishing their meals under the outdoor cabana of a small restaurant. I was holding the toy-water-pistol camera, strapped around my neck, when shouting children suddenly surrounded me. They were pointing at the camera, wanting me to photograph them. I decided I would play with the children, pretending to take their pictures, and then squirt them. But before I knew it, a crowd of families had formed around me. Growing frightened, I tried telling them in my broken Spanish that it was only a toy, but soon an extended family was positioning itself for a picture. The old grandfather, grandmother, and mother seated themselves on small stools in the front with the little children on the ground at their sides. The father orchestrated the older children, young men, and young women in the two back rows.

Soon a large crowd had gathered around to watch. I heard Hamm shout out, "No, Prudy!" He had been separated from me by the growing crowd and was watching in disbelief. Afterward he said if he'd been able to get closer, he would never have let it get that far out of hand. Shouting and waving his hands, he signaled for me to run, but I felt my only way out was to pretend I was taking a picture. The group of spectators would never know. I coolly lifted and pointed my camera, and there was a moment of hushed silence as the family sat grinning.

I slowly pressed the button down, foolishly thinking that pushing it gradually would prevent the water from squirting out. Quite the contrary, a perfectly formed spout of water sailed through the air and onto the shirt of the grand patriarch seated in the front row. There was an immediate outburst of rage, everyone screaming at once. Hamm broke through the crowd, pulling me toward him. Ashamed, I broke loose from his grip and bolted back to the table where my father, siblings, and mother sat, oblivious, peacefully drinking their tea and coffee in the café at the end of block.

The father, grandmother, mother, and much of the crowd followed, yelling and shouting Spanish expletives at us. They told my parents, who both spoke Spanish, and my mother was furious. Without even waiting to hear my version of events, she ripped the camera from my neck, angrily telling Mia and Johnny that this happened on their watch. I was made to apologize to each member of the large family, while my father begged forgiveness and gave them money, which seemed to settle the matter. I was never again allowed on set in Denia.

Barbara returned, and the summer continued on lazily and uneventfully. When it was time to leave, my mother decided we should take a car trip to Valencia and Barcelona and then on through to the Catholic pilgrimage village of Lourdes at the base of the Pyrenees Mountains in France. She said it would be a trip we would remember for the rest of our lives. She had always wanted to go to Lourdes, and she also loved flamenco dancing and guitar, which we would see in both Spanish cities. Our mother decided to invite her mother, our Granny from Ireland, to join us for the last leg of the journey from Barcelona to the holy village of Lourdes. Even though Granny could be a difficult personality, my mother thought she might be on good behavior, being a devout Catholic on her way to Lourdes. She also felt it had been too long since we had seen her. We were excited but a little wary, for Granny *could* be unpredictable.

Our journey up the coast through Valencia and into Barcelona was beautiful. My mother loved the architecture by the Moors, so prevalent throughout Spain. After leaving Barcelona, we stopped alongside the road to picnic. We laid out our meal under a tree on a lovely green pasture. One of my siblings mentioned how stupid the squirting-camera incident was in Denia. I knew I should ignore it, but I couldn't. It was still too contentious a matter for me to let go. The argument grew out of proportion as I angrily defended myself. My mother suddenly became unusually silent. I don't think we had ever before seen our mother so angry. She remained silent the entire remainder of the day. Following her lead, the others were all furious with me, and even Barbara gave me the cold shoulder.

But Granny, who could be very mean at such times, went in for the kill. "You are a thoughtless, selfish girl. How could you do this to your mother? It's no wonder she is fed up with you and sending you off to boarding school."

"What do you mean? I am not going to boarding school!" I shot back.

"Yes, your mother is sending you to boarding school."

"She is not!"

"She is!"

"She is not!" I looked to my mother for help. "You are not sending me to boarding school are you, Mummy?"

My mother stared ahead and said, softly, "Yes."

I was devastated, not knowing how to respond. The other children just sat sullenly, looking away. Granny continued, "Yes, she is fed up with especially you." I looked around, hoping for support, but everyone remained close-lipped. I wanted to cry, but I stayed silent. "Well, we've finally quieted her," Granny's words trailed.

We continued our drive north along the Costa Brava coastline. I was glued to my station at the window, hoping to escape the hurtful notions within the car, while peering out reflectively on a fleeting world unlike anything I had known. We stopped at a seaside inn. It was lovely, situated on a large cliff that dropped steeply to the sea. At dinner, we ran into an American family of four, whom we had met in Benidorm. Coincidentally they, too, were staying at the cliff-top inn. There were two girls, one Patrick's age and the other Mia's. All of us were friends with the girls, Becky and Kathy. The family was very friendly and happy to meet up with us so unexpectedly. The adults sat for drinks and continued talking until late in the evening.

While it was still early enough that there was plenty of sunlight, fresh and exhilarated by the sea air, the two girls and I went exploring. Mia, deep into *Wuthering Heights* by Emily Brontë, would not budge. No amount of pleading from us deterred her from her reading. So Kathy and I, following her older sister Becky through a vineyard, suddenly heard and saw several big dark barking dogs aggressively running toward us. We raced, screaming through the vineyard and out to the rocks along the cliff's edge. Fortunately, someone called the dogs off at the last minute.

Becky climbed up the cliff ahead of Kathy and me. The climb was precarious and very difficult. Suddenly, Becky announced she could go no higher. We had to retreat. As we proceeded to retrace our path, the danger of our situation became apparent. Climbing up had been extremely challenging, but going back appeared impossible. We had climbed up by leaping over distances onto small rock ledges, where we could catch hold of slim overhead rocks to keep our balance as we landed. But jumping back over and downward to the same slim ledges with nothing to grab and hang onto was something quite different. Three hundred feet below, the sea crashed wildly. Falling onto the jagged rocks that lined the shore meant certain death.

Since I had been trailing slowly behind, when Becky realized what she was up against, she yelled hysterically for me to go back for help. She and Kathy had climbed a good distance above me. While I had only one such leap of faith, so to speak, to freedom, they had many more. They pleaded with me, and we were all crying. I hadn't been to confession in months, so my soul was riddled with mortal sins. I tried to explain that I was not merely facing death but eternal damnation. I just couldn't risk it. Becky screamed at me, "You shall die anyway if you do nothing! We shall all die!" Convinced, I slowly, in sheer terror, scaled my way back down for help.

Racing back to the inn, I passed through the vineyard, unafraid of the barking dogs that tore after me biting at my legs and heels. By comparison to being stranded high on the seaside cliffs, being bitten seemed trite. Arriving at the inn and a table full of parents, out of breath, I hysterically told of the girls precariously perched on the side of the high rocks. The peaceful group of adults seated together enjoying the glow of their wine suddenly came to life. Soon a posse of several handymen who worked the grounds came to our aid with big bright flashlights, ropes, and ladders. I was told to stay back at the inn, as were all the children. About an hour after my escape, at the top of the cliff on a piece of property overlooking the ocean just above where the girls were stranded, bright spotlights guided dark descending ropes lowered to rescue Becky and Kathy. My heroic actions were heralded by all, even Granny. My mother rewarded me with a warm proud forgiving embrace, along with a delicious cup of hot chocolate.

The next morning we left the inn early to travel inland, deep into the Pyrenees Mountains. It was my turn to ride behind the powder-blue Cadillac, in the Karmann Ghia with my mother. After some time, I mustered the courage to tell her I did not deliberately squirt the Spanish family. She said she knew but that I should never have let it get so far. Everyone had said the same thing. I wanted to blurt back that it wasn't so easy, but the finality in her tone of voice silenced me. Confused, I remained quiet and pondered how I could have righted the misdeed. If I had refused to take the family's picture or ran away, wouldn't they have been very insulted? This meant I *had* to take their picture, only I should have pretended to push the camera's button. That way no one would have been hurt. This was the only solution I could come up with, but it bothered me that it probably would not have been my parents'.

At midday, we picnicked under a weeping willow in a wet sloping meadow alongside the road at the base of the mountains. That night, we stopped at a ski lodge. It was off-season, but the area was beautiful with long hilly stretches of bright-green grass. Several ski lifts led high up to the peaks of the surrounding mountains and stretched low over the rolling grasses. Early the next morning, for a couple hours before continuing to Lourdes, we had great fun riding the lifts.

After a half day of driving, navigating the winding mountain roads became more and more treacherous. I wished I were still in my mother's car. Vicente's reckless approach to the unremittingly sharp bends in the road was to honk his horn and accelerate. Temporarily blinded by hairpin turns and with no regard for oncoming cars, he jeopardized our lives several times when our car was almost forced over the side of the steep mountain cliffs. Granny blamed it on hubris resulting from driving a big Cadillac in a poor nation of tiny cars.

Finally arriving in Lourdes, we were not disappointed by what we saw. Even though for me, at this age, the National Shrine Grotto of Our Lady of Lourdes was to be more a spectacle than a spiritual center, the phenomena of its all-pervasive rituals and ceremonies, and the thousands of worshipping believers, did not let me down.

It was a pageant of unusual and fantastic sights. At night, long processions of people carried lit candles and sang "Ave Maria," winding their way dramatically through the small town before emptying into one large open square at the base of the grand luminescent Basilica of the Rosary. The rising towers of the Basilica of the Immaculate Conception soared behind.

Among the pilgrims were hundreds of strange and exotic orders of nuns and priests, in every kind of habit possible, from all over the world. Fascinating recluse orders, covered in veils, never showing their faces, knelt all day praying in the many hidden and obscure side chapels diffused throughout the great basilicas. Different monasteries and convents lined the river facing the grotto and its basilicas. A continuous hum of prayers, whispered, spoken, and chanted, permeated the atmosphere. The streets of the town and its large square were filled with colorful Gypsy vendors who brazenly pushed their wares, souvenirs of all types such as plastic containers in an assortment of shapes and sizes to hold the holy water of Lourdes; all different kinds and sizes of rosaries, crucifixes, and medallions; silver spoons, porcelain bowls, plates, and small shot glasses painted with pictures of the grotto; candles of every type, size, and shape; and various statues and pictures of Our Lady.

For Granny, this *was* heaven. She adopted an air of great piety that lasted the whole time we were there. For two days, we listened to her mutter the Rosary nonstop under her breath. Our days in Lourdes started early. First, we went to six o'clock mass in the Basilica of the Rosary. The towering basilicas were built on the hill atop the sacred grotto, the vibrant heart of Lourdes, where the Virgin Mary is said to have appeared. After mass, we rushed to wait in long lines for up to several hours to pass through the area of the grotto. The water flowing from the grotto was deemed miraculous, mysteriously materializing after the Virgin's appearance. Once in the hallowed grotto, we waited in more lines for several hours to bathe in its revered baths.

Every kind of invalid imaginable was lined up in multiple rows before the grotto, which faced out onto the rapid-flowing river

Gave de Pau. Languages from all over the world could be heard. An impressive array of thousands of crutches and wheelchairs from those who were healed were hung from the top to the bottom of the tall outer stone walls leading to the grotto. They also were hung by the hundreds along the stone sides of the hill along the pathway from the grotto leading to the baths. We visited and bathed in its waters twice. Barbara, an Episcopalian, did not participate during the days, which were excruciatingly hot. By the second day, I think all of us, including Granny, envied Barbara. But she participated in the evenings, when we marched along in procession with several thousand people, holding our small lit candles and singing "Ave Maria" at the top of our lungs. This was particularly moving, especially for Granny, whose high-pitched Irish voice wailed well above practically all the others.

After leaving Lourdes, we made our way back to Madrid, but I have no recollection of how. It could have been by plane or car. We stayed at the Castellano Hilton once again. Having come full circle, it was a fitting closure to our time in Spain. In the next days, we would head for London, new schools, and new life. I immediately tried to meet up with Lizzy, but she was visiting her grandparents in the United States. Granny was leaving to go back to Ireland. The evening before her departure, my mother took us all out to eat at an expensive restaurant for a final farewell dinner for Granny.

Granny was in rare form, highly amusing and full of conversation. In the afternoon, for her return to Ireland, she had dyed her hair—what was left of it—orange. Back when she visited us in the United States, she had used too strong a dye on her hair with disastrous results. Most of it fell out and what was left turned green. Now, her mostly bald head consisted of little blotches of hair, like separate little islands scattered across her skull. Tonight she had taken great care to comb strands over each patchy part, giving somewhat of an appearance of one unified head of hair. As she entered the room, we could practically hear her personality crackling.

With the reality of leaving Spain, boarding school looming—for all the older children, not just me—and the uncertainty of a new life in London, we all felt glum. Granny immediately noticed and said the occasion called for her shrieking laugh, which worked every time. We had never heard it before, but according to her, she had been performing it successfully for many years for her Irish grandchildren. We children were dressed up, waiting in the small living room of our hotel suite for our parents to arrive. Granny stood in the middle of the room, beginning what she aptly described as "shrieking." I wondered where the "laugh" was. Her horrible screeching brought me through all the levels of emotion I felt for her, mostly negative. It started off harsh and grating, and grew in pitch and abrasiveness until it became so jarring it was almost unbearable. Yet she continued. *What is she doing?* Suddenly, something in me snapped, and it all became insanely ridiculous. Yes, it was funny and mad, quite mad. All of us laughed and laughed and laughed.

By the end of our meal, the magic of Granny's absurd performance had worn off and we were once again faced with the gravity of our farewell meal. Granny's continued gaiety and obvious elation at returning home stood in stark contrast to our feelings of grief, making it hard to mask a growing irritation toward her. Along with the sadness of our imminent separation, apprehension regarding the new lives we were about to face was palpable. We were traveling to reside in a country we had never been to before, living under conditions we never imagined.

On our return to the hotel from the restaurant, no one spoke. I looked at Granny, who was staring out the cab window. I wondered if she finally realized her gaiety was no longer appropriate. But then she spoke, "We mustn't be glum. We shall all see each other again soon. Let's plan to reunite for Christmas."

Thinking this a good idea, I gave a hearty "yes!" But everyone else, lost in their own thoughts, responded only halfheartedly. This was the last we would spend any significant amount of time with Granny. We saw her briefly in Ireland the following summer. She died from pneumonia in 1963. That last night in Spain, still a little annoyed with Granny, no one gave her the heartfelt goodbye she deserved. We hugged her briefly, maybe a bit awkwardly, before she went off to her room to sleep. We didn't see her the next morning; she had an early flight.

Steffi, Tisa, and I were left with Barbara to stay on longer in Madrid while all the others went on ahead to London. We made the best of our last week in Spain by boating in the park, drinking chocolate milkshakes, enjoying hot cocoa with marshmallows before bed, taking advantage of the best room service had to offer, eating at the expensive hotel restaurant, and having afternoon tea and scrumptious desserts at the small Sun Terrace Bar and Restaurant. Barbara brought out our new luggage, which had been stowed away in hotel storage for the last months. I was still excited by the sight of my brand-new set of plaid luggage and all the new clothes.

Steffi and Tisa were going to a day school in London, with Barbara and my mother taking care of them. We would all be wearing uniforms. Mine was for my boarding school in Surrey. Barbara showed us how to wear our new uniforms and which sweaters best fit under our school jackets. As a surprise, Barbara bought each of us, ordered fresh from Scotland, bright happy new hot-water bottles for our feet in what she called "the damp English cold." These were novel to us, but she assured us we would need them in our new environment. Mine was light blue with a thick fuzzy velour covering. Barbara was right. In the months ahead, I became very attached to my hot-water bottle.

TISA, STEFFI, PRUDENCE, JOHNNY
AND MIA IN BENIDORM 1958

MAUREEN WITH GRANNY IN
FRONTOFSKILODGEONOURWAY
TO LOURDES IN 1958

ten

Cloistered Life: Catholic Boarding School

The morning of our departure from Spain came all too quickly as we rushed to meet our flight. We boarded the plane with heavy hearts and a growing feeling of foreboding. Watching the stewardess pull the plane's hatch shut, sealing us off from our life of the last eight months and into the fuselage of the plane aptly reflected the finality of our ensuing fate. At the same time, we were children, so there was an undeniably mounting feeling of wonderment. Steffi and I sat behind Barbara and Tisa. As the plane's propellers roared, shaking my entire being to its core, Steffi's and my eyes locked, frozen in what seemed to be a timeless moment of profound excitement…or was it intense horror? It didn't seem to matter—at this point, it was hard to sort the difference between the two.

Our flight attendant was warm and motherly, in a way only the Spanish could be. She tucked us in with blankets and pillows, and loaded us up with snacks. We had a layover in Paris, during which she brought us delicious French pastries and an assortment of colorful candies wrapped in every kind of paper imaginable. We gorged ourselves. Steffi showed more restraint than I did and reminded me we weren't supposed to eat partially wrapped or un-wrapped candies. Barbara warned us many times to be careful with these, always making certain of the purity of everything we ate. Nevertheless I indulged freely.

We landed, with a couple of hard thuds, at Heathrow Airport in London. Barbara, in possession of our passports and paperwork, navigated us through customs. We were met outside by our new chauffeur Freddie, who drove us to the Park Lane Hotel across from Hyde Park. Freddie was not at all like Vicente. He was very savvy and perceptive, never missing anything that went on. I felt he was almost a spy in the house. He and Barbara spent an inordinate amount of time together, playing cribbage and gin rummy.

Mia and I went to the same boarding school almost immedi-ately upon arriving in London, but Barbara and the younger chil-dren and my mother lived in the hotel until just before Christmas. My father stayed at a London men's club, and Johnny was already at boarding school. I felt for him, being all by himself. Patrick had joined the US Merchant Marines, and Michael was attending col-lege in Washington, DC.

After Spain, everything in London appeared drab, colorless, and covered with filmy soot. As we ventured farther out of the city into Surrey, on our drive to Marymount International School, ev-erything looked so green—the trees dominated the landscape. We pulled into a long winding driveway that led to a lovely old stone English manor house covered with ivy. The front door was wood-en, with a huge stone overhang supporting the rooms above. This was the main school building, housing the middle school, college students, and dining room. I would be staying here. The chapel, high school, and gymnasium were off to its right. Mia would stay in the high-school dormitories just down the street.

Although the main building was huge and old, it was warm and welcoming. There was a happy air about it. Still, knowing it was to be my home for the next year, I was overwhelmed with home-sickness. Mia was swept off to her dorm room by a small group of chattering girls her age. My room was very large, with four beds. It brought to mind the room Wendy, John, and Michael shared in

Peter Pan. I did not see Mia again until mealtime in the downstairs dining room, where she sat surrounded by the same chattering girls. We barely had a chance to exchange a few quick glances before the bell rang and everyone was ushered back to their living quarters.

This was the first time Mia and I had been separated from our family for any extended time. As I lay in bed overcome with sadness and homesickness, I felt a sudden intense burning followed by a deep rumbling in my stomach. I raced to the toilet, where I remained for the rest of the night...and much of the next two months. Steffi also was up all night compulsively vomiting, but her condition lasted for only several days. She and I had picked up amoebas in the candies we ate on the flight over! I had severe dysentery and lived for the next three weeks in unbearable pain.

The nuns moved me to a huge spacious room with a large canopy bed. It was a bright room with tall windows and lots of light. The walls were trimmed in mahogany, with elegant furniture to match, and an exquisitely intricate blue oriental carpet graced the floor. But I hardly could appreciate anything, as I was in and out of consciousness in a delirium of pain. The nuns showered kindness and attention on me. Mia was put in the room with me on a small sofa bed for a couple of weeks. Just knowing she was there made a huge difference. She sat quietly by the side of my bed so that I could turn my head and see her reading. All the while I lay exhausted and motionless, unable to communicate with her for fear and terrible dread of activating the ravaging torrent of agonizing convulsions that relentlessly consumed my body.

As the burning spasmic storms subsided, leaving me an hour or two before their return, I reached out to Mia as if she were my savior, imploring her to rescue me from this hell. She climbed into my bed and held me. Hugging me with all her might, she cried and cried with me. As I recovered, with a bright light from outside streaming in, I experienced a happiness and contentment I had not felt for a long time. The room was filled with gentleness and softness, supporting and nourishing me. There was a purity here that I had never experienced before.

Our lives almost immediately took the shape of the nuns' lives. Every morning, we were wakened for six o'clock mass, which was sung in Latin. Each Wednesday afternoon, we attended benediction, also sung. After morning mass, we had breakfast and then religion class for an hour, followed by our daily studies.

Most of the nuns were forgettable, but a few were holy terrors, and a couple were wonderful. Their influence on me was profound. One in particular was adored by all of us. Her voice rang out celestially above all the others in mass every morning. She was beautiful, with a beaming smiling round face and complexion of a redhead. She was young and fun. Her whole demeanor radiated contagious serenity and spiritual bliss. Due to her countenance, a deep yearning for a spiritual life was kindled in all of us. She was the first person I consciously encountered who lived spirituality and made it real. She was my heroine and role model. We all wanted to be nuns, to be just like her.

My roommate Sally and I were especially ambitious in this cause, inspired by legendary stories told to us of great monks and saints who wore horsehair shirts, slept with crowns of thorns on their heads, and whipped themselves relentlessly to discipline their hopelessly deluded minds and bodies into submission. Rumor spread quietly among us about the existence of nettle bushes growing wild somewhere in the back of the enormous manicured gardens behind the school buildings. One afternoon after making me take a vow of absolute secrecy, Sally took me to the growth of wild bushes. I don't know how she found them, but I suspect her older sister, who was in Mia's class, was the source. I never knew for sure. To become a real saint, we had to abide by Jesus's rule to "not let your left hand know what your right hand is doing." Otherwise, one could become a victim of pride.

Almost daily in the late afternoon, after study hall, Sally and I stealthily slipped out of the building and raced toward the wild nettle bushes. While carefully guarding each other, removing our uniform jackets and shirts, we began what became an almost daily ritual of pressing the fine hair-like structures of the nettle leaves against our naked skin, burning and filling our upper arms, chests, and backs with numerous raised red welts. Because of the secrecy surrounding this ritual, I don't know how many of the girls partook, but I expect there were many more.

The nuns eventually found out, and the bushes were removed. A great disappointment fell over the more fanatical girls, myself included. In our race for sainthood, we knew we would probably never find a replacement quite as effective. The nuns told us this was not what God intended when He spoke of penance. But that hardly convinced us after being told for years the stories of the lives of saints and what they did to themselves. Later, we learned from sneaking into their rooms that some of these nuns slept with crowns of thorns on their heads and wore prickly under vests of horsehair. We were punished for our daily jaunts to the forbidden nettle bushes by being grounded in the afternoons and Saturdays. During this time, while everyone else played outside, we had to stay in the sewing room and work on long sewing projects. But this punishment, hard as it was, barely held ground next to sitting in class all day with the sore welts left by the nettles.

The habits the nuns wore were entirely new to me. Their faces were enveloped on each side by what could only be called blinders—as if someone took two pieces of white cardboard and lined the sides of their faces, meeting at the tips of their foreheads and chins. They protruded out about three inches on each side, obstructing all possible peripheral vision in either direction. A black veil was draped over. The obstructed side vision, of course, favored the students who quickly adopted behavior patterns unknown to the partially blinded nuns. Instead of "Sister," these nuns were called "Mother." The Reverend Mother required a curtsy before being addressed.

Also new to me was a uniform that included shoes almost identical to the nuns'. They were black lace-up leather shoes with heavy heeled soles. The heel was thick and somewhat stacked. If I placed the heel down first, the front sole automatically snapped to the ground with a loud crack. Of course, this became the only way I would walk. I got so good at it that as the front sole came down I could give it a quick twist inward that made it seem even more delightful. I ambulated loudly around the school, annoying everyone, particularly the nuns and older girls.

As time wore on, I adjusted to my new life. My best friend Sally was correct in predicting that I would never want to leave. She and I had a natural kinship I don't think I ever felt again with anyone else. We were both a little nutty and as such were the favorites of the "prepsies," or middle-schoolers. We each wore glasses and were extremely skinny with dark short hair. Sally's hair stuck out and up, like straw. She was brutally honest and hilarious, with acutely accurate observations. She could be mean, but was mostly just funny.

On a weekend night in early October, Sally and I left the other girls, who were telling ghost stories, to return to our room. Turning off the lights, we told our own stories while playing 45-rpm records. Sally put on a very sad song, and we hugged each other, swaying to the music as our eyes welled up with tears. At that moment, several nuns entered the room and turned on the lights abruptly. We immediately felt their sense of shock. Awkwardly, Sally and I untangled our embrace and felt strangely embarrassed. Judging by their reactions, we must have been guilty of something quite hideous. Ashamed and in silence, Sally and I parted, turned off the record player, and got ready for bed. The nuns said nothing but stood watching us for a long time. Turning, they finally left. Sally and I went to bed and never mentioned it again.

Our prepsie classroom was next to the nuns' quarters, with a door leading to their private entrance. The fear of God, well instilled, kept us from even desiring to go near it. I was often noisy after hours, keeping the other girls up as I whispered and giggled late into the night. The nuns were fed up with me. One evening after they had had enough, it was decided I would be isolated from the other girls. Hoping to humiliate me into proper behavior, I was put into the classroom to sleep until I learned to behave myself. In the lonely isolation of my new bedroom, that single door leading to the nuns' quarters grew in size. I tried it once, and it was locked.

I decided to try it again earlier in the day, in the late afternoon, when it was very safe since the nuns would be in chapel. I quietly turned the handle, and the door opened to reveal a well-lit hallway containing a few small sparse bedrooms off of it. To the immediate left was a small stairway. I entered the first bedroom on my right. I remember a lone bed with a white bedspread and a window to the right. On the pillow of the bed was a crown of thorns, similar to what Jesus had worn. I suddenly heard the rustle of nuns' robes coming up the stairs. I was out of there in a flash and back in the classroom, shaken but happy that I had not been caught. I never went back, for my curiosity never again outweighed the fear of the consequences, whether they be heavenly or earthly.

The curriculum of the school included the usual academic staples as well as italic handwriting, sewing, and gym. I spent most of my time learning to write italics. This was because I was left-handed, and the nuns required that I learn to write with my right hand. Most of my learning this entire year was spent trying to master right-handedness. Mia and Barbara claimed the reason I was left-handed was I figured out I could attract more attention this way. When I told the nuns this theory, they agreed.

Mia and I adapted to our new life surprisingly quickly. Our mother's letters were getting further apart. I supposed it was because she could tell from my brief notes and Mia's longer letters that we loved it there. If we heard more from her, it was mostly through the Reverend Mother.

Just before Halloween, Reverend Mother called me into her office. Her manner was different than usual. Instead of being typically strict and abrasive, she and her assistant Mother Charles, who was always at her side, were warm and welcoming. Suspicious, I was taken aback, delighted but uneasy with their behavior. Reverend Mother began talking philosophically about life. I didn't understand what she was trying to say—she made no sense. She spoke of my parents and how they wished they could be here with us now. She talked about Mia waiting for me out in the hallway and then more philosophy. She took my hand ever so kindly, saying she knew I was strong and that I would take this in the proper way. She then proceeded to tell me my brother Michael had been killed in an airplane accident over Los Angeles. Our parents were in California now.

"You are wrong!" I shouted out, surprising even myself.

"No, no, no," Reverend Mother quietly responded, gently leading me toward the hallway where Mia waited. Mia and I hugged each other tightly. Mia appeared strong, but I knew she was taking it much harder than I was. She had been very close to Michael. He called her his "mouse." Mia and I were led around in a daze and fed delicious scones and tea in Reverend Mother's special meeting room. Mother Charles tried engaging us in light conversation, and I struggled futilely to focus on what she was saying. Once again, Mia amazed me with her poise as she responded to question after trivial question.

A special mass was given in our brother's honor to bless his soul. The whole student body was there. I walked down the center aisle of the small chapel as "Ave Maria" was sung. The voice of the young beautiful nun we all loved rang out as always above all the others. Its clarity and poignancy were unbearable. I looked over at Mia, whose face was ashen. She was seeing far more than this moment. All the happy secure years she had known her entire life, with one stroke were over. She was facing an unfamiliar emptiness. It would take years for both of us to fill the abyss inside. I felt dread slowly seep into the core of my being, as if this loss were merely an omen, a precursor, to many more dark years ahead. I felt as if I were an outsider looking into a world in which I no longer trusted. Mia and I were not just mourning the death of our brother. We were mourning our own deaths, the unbearable loss of hope.

Mia was deeply shaken. Sally's older sister Piper heard Mia's muffled sobs at night as she cried into her pillow. It was not the same for me. I only cried at the special mass held for my brother, and that was only when "Ave Maria" was sung. What was strange was that I didn't shed another tear for many weeks. I just could not grasp it all. As a result, I felt nothing. I *tried* to be sad, but every time I thought about never seeing my brother again, a part of me refused to believe it. Nothing seemed real.

I wondered if something was wrong with me, maybe that lobotomy. Everyone was being so extra kind to me. How could I let them know I felt nothing? I felt quite guilty. Sensing a growing distance between myself and others, I felt alone and helpless. One night I was awake, thinking about what Sally's sister said about Mia weeping into her pillow, and I couldn't bear it anymore. I decided to confess my ugly truth, but whom could I tell? Something froze deep inside of me, making it impossible to tell my dark secret. Mia was crying, but I could not cry.

That night, Sally sensed my predicament. She asked me if I was OK. I blurted out that I felt different than everyone else. I couldn't cry or feel sad. I didn't even miss my brother. To my astonishment, she said she and everyone knew this. She told me to talk to her sister Piper. When I met Piper and confessed my feelings, she told me there was nothing unusual about it. It was normal for someone my age. I didn't understand. She continued explaining that I was still a child and children cannot react to things they do not understand. I responded that she was a child, too, but she didn't agree.

At fourteen, she was old enough to realize about death, she went on to explain, and that she wished she were younger like me at age ten years old. I asked her, if this were the case, then why is everyone treating me so extra kindly when I'm the one who doesn't feel anything? She said that is part of growing older, too, because when people don't know their loss, it makes others feel even sadder for them. I didn't understand this at all and told her I would have to think very hard about it. She assured me I would understand everything in about two years. Drawing me close to her, she said, "This is why we all love you so much." I felt strangely forgiven and at peace for the first time in what seemed an eon.

When Mia and I left school to go "home" for Thanksgiving vacation, I realized how fortunate we were to be in boarding school where we didn't have to witness our parents' suffering. Our family was still living in London's Park Lane Hotel, my two younger sisters down the hall from my mother's apartment suite. I came out of their quarters to go to lunch with Barbara, the chauffeur Freddie, and my two younger sisters. Then I heard a blood-curdling scream, which continued for some time, coming from my mother's apartment at the end of the hallway. From the midst of this wailing, I could decipher my mother trying to articulate my deceased brother Michael's name. It was as if she were seeing his ghost.

She suddenly quieted down. I then heard the distant sound of my mother sobbing loudly and then yelling desperately for Patrick, who raced out of his room and slipped into our mother's apartment, gently closing the door behind him. When I frantically turned to Barbara and Freddie for a response, I was stunned to see them continuing their conversation and nonchalantly walking to the elevator. Running toward them, I tried to engage them, laughing and crying at the same time. I remember watching myself and not understanding. Freddie grabbed me, shook me, and slapped me while saying, "Get a hold of yourself!"

"Why is Patrick going into her room?" I shouted.

"She will only see Patrick."

After lunch, I sneaked in to see my mother. She was lying on the bed. Crossing the room, I leaned in to kiss her most delicate Irish face, which was swollen red. She seemed barely conscious, her breathing so subtle as to nearly have stopped altogether. A look of horror must have passed over my face, because Barbara, who had followed me into the room, reached deftly across the bed and quickly scooped me into her strong Scottish arms and whispered into my ear, "No, Prudy, she is just sleeping."

Happily we returned to school, where everybody and everything were the same as we had left them. All of us, including our friends, seemed relieved to be back in the security of this predictable setting. Sally felt the same as I did—we were delighted to be reunited. We wouldn't have to leave again until just before Christmas. I thought that perhaps Mia and I were not the only ones whose lives felt incomplete or somehow unreal when not here. The more time I spent at the school the more comfortable I felt, and the nuns said my wild streak was settling down.

When Christmas vacation came, Mia and I were scheduled this time to go to a new "home," a rented four-story brownstone in Chelsea, London. Steffi and Tisa were already happily moved in on the third floor, and my mother had the top floor. Barbara's room and the playroom were on the second floor. The playroom was continuously inhabited by Barbara and Freddie, the chauffeur. They played cards nonstop, chattering and laughing into the wee hours of every morning. Part of me resented that Barbara's attention was so thoroughly usurped by Freddie. He was bossy and always had an opinion, and Barbara ran everything by him. I asked Steffi about it, and she said they were in love. I was shocked. I had never imagined Barbara that way—it was almost like imagining a nun getting married.

There was a tangible sadness that Christmas. We went to midnight mass at the Church of Our Most Holy Redeemer & St. Thomas More. My mother's body, bent over in prayer, quivered and shook as she silently wept. Halfway through, my father slipped off toward a side chapel. Grabbing Barbara's attention, I pleaded to go with him. She nodded her approval, and I pursued him through the back of the church. The historic old church was particularly beautiful this Christmas night, lit by flickering candles that softly and gently played upon its whitewashed walls. The candles peacefully popped and crackled in the serene silence permeated by years of continuous prayer.

Trailing behind him, I followed my father into a tiny chapel. Unaware of my presence, he knelt and fervently prayed before a stark crucifix. His head was resting in his hands, his brow pinched in intense concentration. As I watched, I had the thought that this is a man who knows death. The shape of his bent-over body and manner in which he held himself portrayed him as if he were burdened by an enormous weight. A sudden and terrible sadness enshrouded me.

The image of my father alone in unbearable pain emblazoned a hole in my heart that physically hurt, leaving me with a sense of emptiness and desolation I had never before encountered. I remembered Piper's words to me after my brother's death. She had almost envied my childhood mindset, expressing that I did not feel the pain adults did but that I would someday know it. I was certain now I knew it. I watched frozen for some time, absorbing the situation as if through osmosis.

Letting it set in that my father was a broken man, perhaps irreparably, I wanted to reach out to him and hold him in my arms.

But even if I had stepped into adulthood, I also recognized I still had one foot lingering in childhood. One annoyed look or word from him could cut me to my core; I was too fragile. Instead, I vowed to never again blame him for being incapable of taking care of us and sending us to boarding school. I swore also to always be thoughtful, kind, generous, and sensitive toward him for the rest of his days. I hated seeing him the way I had that Christmas night. At the same time, I was grateful because I would never resent parting from him again. I would always know he loved me.

The remainder of the school year passed by largely uneventfully but happily, with running competitions, gymnastics events, Easter processions, and May Day festivities. We loved our new life and dreamed of when we would return the next year. By the end of that first year, I had become extremely religious. Making morning mass was of utmost importance, giving me great pleasure. It was my special time, some much-needed solitude. I kindled a serious desire to devote my life to God. Through those quiet early-morning services, something within me was profoundly stirred.

Even so, I was frequently called into Reverend Mother's office for various disruptive behaviors, such as shooting water out of the snout of my pink rubber piggy bank, throwing spitballs, shooting rubber bands, or cracking ever-forbidden chewing gum between my teeth. Reverend Mother was stern and strict, making it clear that if not for my family situation, I would have been asked to leave. As the year drew to a close, my heart was heavy since my return was by no means guaranteed.

One day Reverend Mother called me into the office, and I was very frightened. Smiling, she said she was happy to inform me my behavior had improved enough so that it was no longer an obstacle to my returning the next year. I breathed an enormous sigh of relief. According to Mia, the real reason I was invited back was because our father donated a generously large sum of money for construction of the new gymnasium.

eleven

Summer in the Country

Mia, Johnny, and I spent that summer of 1959 on a farm in the lowlands of England in Dorset, very near the heathlands. We worked hard all summer, helping with general farm duties, mostly cleaning stalls. There were about two hundred milk cows and several horses. We observed the birth of a calf, took care of numerous chicks, and witnessed the mating of a bull with a cow. A few days after arriving, Mia and I were given our own Sherwood Forest ponies, and Johnny a great huge swayback farm horse, to care for and ride. Mia had the mother of my pony, who was appropriately named "Impudence." I did not like Impudence much, mostly because she did not like me or anyone else. She was a mean-spirited pony whose greatest joy was to either throw me from her back or turn and take a good nip from my thigh. The nuns at school had often called me "Impudence," and I finally got to know what it meant. I knew nothing about karma at that time, but I was certainly getting it back in spades.

An American man named Mark and his English wife Laura owned the farm. Mark was irritable and mean, but Laura was always good-natured and nice. Mark didn't care much for Johnny or me, but he liked Mia, constantly pointing her out as an example of good manners and appropriate behavior.

A memorable moment of my life happened on the heath, under a full summer moon. Mark had spoken to us for weeks about taking the horses out to run on the heath. His whole demeanor changed as he spoke of its mist and tumbleweed and how it made something stir in him like nowhere else on earth. It was haunting, he told us, and he always longed to return as soon as he left. He prepared us weeks in advance for our trip. He said even the horses sensed the heath and would become wild and crazy in anticipation. Therefore, he had to prepare us to ride skillfully before he could take us, near the end of our stay.

Finally when the time came, we saddled up and prepared to leave in the evening, under the light of the rising full moon. We felt the horses' excitement growing as we mounted them. They knew where they were going, better than we did. As the horses became increasingly more difficult to control, we headed out with a good hour's ride before reaching the heath. It had just gotten dark, and nature's nightlife was just coming into full swing.

As we neared the heath, a gentle but firm breeze carried the more pungent smells of the flatlands, its heather, and dry scrubs. The wind was warm, passing through our hair and the horses' manes. The horses wanted to run, and soon there would be no containing them. As we reached the edges of the heath, Mark shouted at the top of his lungs to hang onto their manes, raise ourselves up on our stirrups, and forget about controlling them. They'll come around, he said.

Mia and Johnny were already off, bounding ahead of us into the night. I pulled Impudence in with every bit of strength I had, but there was no controlling her now. She took off, encouraged by her mother. Her snorting and panting grew loud, and the wind added to the energy. I quickly became terrified as Impy charged forcefully ahead. Dropping the reins and raising myself up on the stirrups to avoid the rapid pitching and ebbing of her back like a meat grinder, I hung onto her mane for dear life, surrendering to whatever the inevitable held.

Mark initially stayed back with me, but his horse was so fast that soon he disappeared in a cloud of dust. Impy never caught up with the rest, even though she ran as hard as she could for a good half hour and would have continued on for another if Mark hadn't come and taken her reins and pulled her back under control. All the horses were exhilarated by the run. Even though they were sweating and puffing and panting with flared nostrils as they trotted through the brush toward home, their gaits were lighter. Clearly, they were not ready to stop.

As the summer came to a close, I hoped to see more of my mother and was very disappointed when she wrote that she would see me in Ireland at the end of the summer. I left the farm with mixed feelings. It had been such a healthy experience. I loved the lifestyle, getting up at the crack of dawn and tending to animals, even while I had misgivings about Mark's temperament. I was excited to reunite with my younger sisters and mother. We would meet in Ireland.

Much to my surprise, we spent an unexpectedly happy summer's end with our Irish cousins, playing among the hay fields, riding horses, cleaning stalls, and swimming in the ice-cold sea. Even so, the sense of an uncertain future hung heavily over me. We stayed in a tired old country estate set amid rolling hills, a soft patchwork of varying shades of green stretching endlessly into the horizon. Daily we rode horses from the nearby stables. The old manor house we stayed in was neglected, like a forgotten memory crumbling under a cumbersome blanket of rotting thick moss. Its appearance was somber and dank.

Mia, Steffi, Tisa, and I shared a large upstairs bedroom with four dilapidated canopy beds with disconcertingly sunken old mattresses. The walls were dark, covered by archaic wallpaper with patterns and designs too old to define. Centered along the main wall was a fireplace, long in disuse. The ceiling of the once grand bedroom was very high and peaked at its center. Positioned at its topmost sloping sides, framed by broken wooden cupboard-like doors that dangled partially open, were two immensely gaping openings leading to who-knows-where. At night, bats swooped through those holes, flying swiftly over our heads. We heard their high-pitched chirping and slept with the covers over our heads to prevent them from getting caught in our hair.

We ate meals in a charmingly run-down dining room crowned by a stained, crooked-hanging chandelier. The room was freshly painted white, with thin white linen curtains on the windows. There were flowers on little round tables that wore white table-cloths. A happy demeanor brightened this room. A cheerful and friendly elderly woman, whose family had lived in the manor for several generations, was the "help." At mealtime, she and her husband shared the place's history with my mother. In the mornings, we ate eggs fresh from the chickens raised on the estate. When I opened my first boiled egg, I found among bluish and red veins the almost fully formed body of a baby chick. All the previously gooey deliciousness of an egg suddenly took on new meaning. I never enjoyed eating eggs again.

While in Ireland, my mother asked if I wanted to stay on at Marymount or go back to the United States with her and my younger sisters. I wanted to continue at Marymount, but I hesitated. Just before Mia and I left school for the summer, Sally had raced up to me, her eyes popping. She had just heard that next year, at special functions, we would be required to wear stockings and high heels. This was unimaginable to me. I couldn't envision myself displaying my legs in stockings and high heels. I would be mortified. Remembering Sally's words, I told my mother, "No, I want to go back to America."

Barbara flew to Scotland for a much-needed vacation. This time when she returned to the States, she would have a new job with a different family, caring for a four-year-old girl. Parting with Barbara was painful. She had been so much a part of our lives. I had never lived a moment of my life without her being there in some way. That last week together, we kept up a good face for one another, but underneath we all were hurting. Johnny, having known her longer and been her only boy, was in greater pain than

I was. Barbara's departure brought final closure to the world we had inhabited together. She had given every bit of herself to us, and we knew it. Although her bedroom at the airport hotel was separate from ours, I know she also cried that last night. In the morning, her eyes were pink and swollen. She never could hide her emotions—they always revealed themselves in some way.

With great trepidation, I boarded our plane to the United States. I held out hope that the dark cloud hovering since Michael's death would now be lifted. I was wrong. The silence between all of us when we boarded the plane and journeyed back preceded a still darker period yet to come. As the airplane circled in toward landing, a cold chill and deepening dread crawled through me.

twelve

Return to the Unforeseen

We returned to live in the same neighborhood in Beverly Hills, staying with the Roach family while my mother looked for a new home to purchase. It took six months, during which time we rarely saw my father, who stayed in a separate apartment downtown. We were told his work and health warranted his having his own place.

I was set to begin school the day after we arrived, the same one I had attended more than a year and a half earlier. All the same classmates were there, but they were now pubescent teens. Everyone remembered me, as did I them, but I looked them over with strange fascination as they had grown up much faster than I had. Also, I'd forgotten how terminally tan everyone was in California. It looked strange to me, as if they had painted their faces.

Being in an all-girls boarding school in England had not only arrested my social interaction with boys in particular, but it appeared also to have stunted my physical development. Twelve-year-olds looked more to me like seventeen-year-olds. All the girls seemed so adult, wearing brassieres, having complicated curled hairdos, talking of nothing but boys, and going to make-out parties.

I might as well have landed on another planet. My peers were so far advanced, while I, it seemed, had regressed in the sophistication department. Before I left America, I was going steady with a boy from grammar school. I still had his ring. Now, every day after school, I played contentedly with my youngest sister's friends, happily riding my imaginary version of Impudence. I rode the phantom pony back and forth across the back lawn or raced her madly across the front grounds of the homes nearby, jumping hedges, leaping ponds, trotting, cantering, galloping, and running full speed with my small friends watching in total awe.

My classmates, who were once my equals, now looked disdainfully down on me. No one my age wanted to be seen with me. I was a "creep" or "weirdo." Those words still sting when I say them. Perhaps it, too, was karmic, since the two class creeps I would have nothing to do with in my younger years were now my only potential friends. But only one would play with me—the other was too embarrassed. As my self-esteem sank lower, I decided I had to quickly grow up and conform. I stopped riding Impy and turned against my one creepy friend, as well as the other who wasn't having anything to do with me anyway. I changed the way I dressed and wore my hair. To my surprise, an acceptable clique of girls noticed me. They weren't the most popular group, but they were a close second or maybe third.

I was amazed as they actively pursued my friendship. It didn't make sense to me. In my mind, I was still the creep no one wanted to be friends with—but who was I to question? It was enough that they wanted to know me. I think the real reason they now wanted to befriend me was because the boys began to notice me somewhat. To them, I really wasn't so bad. One boy in the popular set told me I was cute.

My confidence grew exponentially but immediately deflated when I heard the boy had said it was too bad I was shaped like a surfboard. When I got wind of this, I went about remedying the situation with some strategically placed foam-rubber cups. My mother and Mrs. Roach looked with astonishment when I entered the house one afternoon with a matronly sized bust.

This heralded the beginning of the most difficult time of my life. In late January, we all moved into our new home about eight blocks away from our original one. Staying with the Roach family had been wonderful, but it was hard to see a new family living in our old home next door.

Our new house never quite felt like home, probably because our life during this period changed and was disrupted in many ways. The house was beautiful. It was a white two-story Spanish stucco house with a thick cement wall in front. Several large magnolia trees led to the front, as you entered through a black wrought-iron gate into a large patio with a lush garden and running fountain.

The living room ran alongside the patio garden. The front door was at the far left end of the garden, opening into a large hallway. The living room was off this hallway on the left side, with the dining room, kitchen, and two separate bedrooms for the boys on the other side. In the center was a staircase leading upstairs to four bedrooms, a large playroom, and a private master suite. This latter was my mother's room. Downstairs, off of the living room, was a sitting room that led into our father's bedroom. At the other far end of the house, toward the street, was the bar in a small den. The backyard was a lot smaller than our previous home, but it had a swimming pool, pool house, and garage.

We were finally all living under one roof again. I had, up to this point, rarely seen much of my father, who was away working most of my life. In this latest phase, he was forced by bad health to watch over us while my mother returned to work. He now lived with us on a full-time basis after years of being largely absent. This period of my life, with him in charge, lasted three years, from age twelve to fifteen. Although this is a relatively small window of time, it was monumental in terms of the adolescent growth taking place as I moved out of childhood.

My father's health had been failing for some time, since Michael's passing in 1958. We all knew our father was dying, for he spoke of his death constantly. He took nitroglycerin, explaining that they were explosive and how his heart would stop if he didn't have these pills to revive it. I was very aware of how frail and fragile his lingering existence was; yet, to my own astonishment, my behavior toward him became increasingly out of control.

All of us children experienced this as we grew tired of hearing about how sick he was. Every complaint was more intolerably boring than the last, until we got up and walked out heartlessly in the middle of his monologues, refusing to let him finish. An hour or two later, remorse would set in. *How could we do such things?* And yet, we did the same thing over and over again. This made matters worse, as our father grappled for attention, only to further alienate himself from us.

When we first moved into the house, my father's health was improving. He still had hope of getting work, and my mother, Patrick, and Mia still lived with us. Dinnertime was the one period each day when the whole family converged at the large dining room table. Our cook served our evening meals promptly at 6:00 p.m., and we had to be washed and dressed nicely. Various current or historical topics were discussed, with my father conducting the flow of conversation from the head of the table. The living room just beyond the dining area was often warmly lit and alive, animated with after-dinner conversation between my father and his old drinking buddies, punctuated by the familiar sounds of ice clinking in cocktail glasses. My father's drinking buddies were still mostly actors and priests from years before.

When my father's health deteriorated and his employment became less certain, my mother left home to work. The somewhat happy lifestyle we had been living for about a year disappeared. The once well-lit living room, so lively with human interaction, was now dismal. All that was left was the terribly lonely figure of a man shuffling about in the large empty darkened portion of the house.

The girls' section of the house was upstairs. My father couldn't climb the stairs because of his heart condition. In the evenings he stood at the bottom of the stairs, and we went down and kissed him good night. During the last year of his life, especially on weekends, he frequently had to shout to us several times to come and kiss him. We were distracted by the television and would go during a commercial break. No matter how long we took, he always waited at the foot of the stairs. We felt terrible but went on doing it. He complained that no one loved him.

One Friday, the night before he died, he waited at the bottom of the staircase for the entire hour of television's *Route 66*, calling out every five to ten minutes. Completely caught up in the show, we forgot about him even when the commercials came. That night after I went to bed and was falling asleep, I suddenly remembered my father. We had forgotten him entirely, as he said we would. I raced through the dark to the bottom of the stairway; he was gone. I went to his room, no light. I felt terrible. I knew what this meant to him. He died the next night.

In the morning I saw him for the last time, since I was going away for the weekend. He was up early, in his robe and slippers. My friend Michelle rang the doorbell to pick me up for a trip to her family's vacation cabin. I rushed to kiss him goodbye. As I was racing away, he mentioned how he had waited an hour the previous night. I told him how sorry I was and then quickly asked him for money for my trip. He gave it to me, but not without guilt-tripping, saying that all he was good for was money. "Of course not," I laughed. After kissing him briskly on the cheek, I rushed off.

Tisa found our father Sunday afternoon, January 28, 1963. The phone receiver was to his ear, as if he were about to make a call. He had a calm peaceful look on his face. Tisa thought he was asleep, but upon seeing that he was not waking, she went quickly for my brother Patrick, who was visiting at the time. (He and Mia had moved to New York City in the summer of 1962 to be with our mother, who was acting in the Broadway show *Never Too Late*.)

My father expected me home on Sunday, but Michelle and I planned to miss a day of school and not come home until Monday. I knew I would not get my father's approval for this, so I waited as late as possible to call from the cabin in Wrightwood, a Mojave Desert ski resort just outside Los Angeles. I would blame Michelle's mother, saying she didn't want to make the long drive back. When we went to dinner at the local restaurant, I called home from the bar. A red rotary-dial phone sat on one end of the bar's countertop for customers to use. Patrick answered the phone, and I asked to speak with our father. He said, bluntly, "Dad's dead."

"You must be kidding!" I replied.

He answered, flatly, "Face it. Dad's dead."

Stunned, I threw the telephone receiver away from me. I didn't want to hear it. Two people behind the bar quickly came to support me, for I must have been collapsing. They consoled me, asked what happened. I couldn't register the profundity of what I had just heard. It seemed odd that the people around me, perfect strangers, could help me. Michelle's mom was alerted, and she came to me. I was in a daze.

Michelle's mother drove us back to the cabin with an unending barrage of forced small talk. I was swept up in a whirlwind, as Michelle and her mother tried to distract me and keep me amused. We had dinner at the cabin, but I could barely eat or talk. We went outside to enjoy the night air and watch as the little lit-up town surrounded by mountains was swallowed by the vast dark desert sky. I felt fortunate to be in the natural majesty of the desert at such a momentous time. Michelle and her mother's constant chatter kept pulling me back with its rise and fall in pitches. I could not keep my attention on what they said. I reacted when the pitch swelled up and got so loud and demanding that it required a grunt or half laugh from me.

Michelle's mother knew my parents for years. She had been married to several well-known movie stars and was typical of a certain ambitious Hollywood woman. She could be described as a "tough broad" who knew her way around. You just knew, upon first sight, you wouldn't want to mess with this woman. Years later I grew fond of her. This particular evening, her generosity and compassion toward me knew no bounds.

When we returned inside the little cabin, Michelle's mother announced that all three of us should get drunk—the occasion warranted it. Michelle beamed, beside herself with excitement. Normally I would have reacted similarly, but now it was the last thing in the world I wanted to do. Three glasses were neatly set in front of us across the kitchen counter as we sat on barstools. The liquor was poured, each glass filled. For every one of my glasses, Michelle drank two as I passed mine her way. She downed each voraciously. Her mother, seeing an empty glass, promptly and repeatedly refilled.

It was not long before my two friends were very drunk. Michelle's mother's incessant talk became endless rambling, changing from sugar-sweet tones—an accomplishment for her with that deep cigarette voice—to mild hysteria to wild youthful candor. At one point, she jumped up from the counter and was once again a young showgirl of nineteen years old. She had the floor and danced the 1920s-style Charleston. She was coy and seductive, full of gaiety, telling us how it once was. Those were the days, she reminisced. People knew how to live then, how to have fun. In no time flat, she was at the counter again, this time next to me.

In drunken intimacy, she asked if I knew what kind of man my father was. Winking her eye with its heavy mascara, implying he had quite a reputation, she slurred, "He was quite a guy around town in his day." Shifting yet again, her words became more blurred as her voice slowed and quieted, full of drama. Her eyes welled up with tears, her arm now around me. Her face came closer, her breath next to mine. "Believe me, sweetie, I know just how you feel." Again, she was off on some other topic, this time with the fervor of youth. Always, she circled back to her basic theme that Michelle and I couldn't really understand how to live life: "They don't make them like they used to, not even my own daughter. You don't know and probably never will know."

Michelle, whose head was silently resting on the countertop, suddenly lunged for the bathroom, leaving a trail of splattering vomit on the floor, couch, and door. Her mother, rudely awakened from her glazed nostalgic dreams, was furious. Michelle didn't vomit quietly, each upchuck coming with a bloodcurdling roar. It was a horrible sound, and her mother was beside herself. She snapped and yelled obscenities in a tough barroom voice. Her language was as foul as it could be, verbally abusive.

Out of the moaning in the bathroom came the roar of Michelle's voice calling her mother a slut, whore, hypocrite, and every foul name she could muster, but she was hardly a match for her mother. She accused her mother of sleeping with any successful man in Hollywood. Michelle surmised her mother had married her father, a homosexual, for his money and fame. It got even uglier. They yelled and shouted, exchanging horrifying barbs between them, bitter and vile. Astounded, I had never witnessed such vulgar violent crudity between two human beings.

It was unbelievable and all intermittently entwined with the most undesirable and disarming howls of Michelle as she violently and dramatically threw up over the toilet, further setting her mother off. It was a human sideshow. Finally, I went to my room and closed the door, leaving them as far behind as I could. They never noticed.

I desperately wanted and needed to process what had just happened—losing my father. I sat on the bed. After such noise for so long, the silence of the desert poured over me, seeping in through the windows and filling the room. The background sounds faded completely. Soothed, I felt isolated but not alone. The isolation consumed me, its stillness quieting me to my core.

I felt a tiny surge of familiarity, first faint but then stronger. It was my father as I had felt him as a young child. A reverence filled me as my experience grew from personal to archetypical. It was my father, all our fathers, all fathers ever, grandfathers, great-grandfathers, and all their children, all people—a sea of humanity, yet one entity, one consciousness, God. It was like a ray of light, rushing, starting very small but quickly growing larger and larger, bursting forth, huge and all-consuming.

I was completely overwhelmed and shaken, yet quiet, ever so content for it had been in sacred silence. I knew in that instant, God, the Holy Spirit, would be with me all my life, silently watching over me. I wanted to weep with gratitude, but the moment was too big for that, even in its gentleness. I felt a lovely peace and safety, for how could I ever forget such an experience? I knew this knowledge would protect and carry me through many challenging times in later life. I was so blessed. I would draw strength from it always. This experience was the gelling of my spiritual side, a part of me that had always lingered just outside my reach. Now I saw it and lived it. But again, it would slip away from me.

After my father's death, my mother came quickly to Los Angeles for the funeral and also left quickly to continue with *Never Too Late*, her Broadway debut. She stayed two or three days, taking Patrick back to New York with her. She decided the younger children should stay where we were and not be put through more changes than absolutely necessary. So we stayed at the house and in our respective schools.

My mother had to find someone to care for us immediately. Barbara came to help, but left after two weeks, saying she could not handle children our age. My mother was furious, calling her "traitor." Fortunately our all-around maid and cook Edna agreed to help the family. Edna was a black woman of about forty-five. She had adored my father, and he loved her, too. So no matter how bad things got, and they did get bad, she was there. We owe a lot to her.

During the time leading up to my father's death, before Mia graduated from high school and went off to live with my mother, we both attended Marymount High School in the Westwood neighborhood of Los Angeles. It was run by the same order of nuns as the boarding school in England, but it was a day school. Mia had grown into an extremely beautiful teenager, especially by California standards in which straight long blond hair was practically a requirement. At our new high school, physical beauty seemed to be everything. Unfortunately for me at this time—braces, freckles, and short dark curly hair—I did not meet even the basic standards. I was skinny and tall, also not appealing. To top it off, I was not an academic star. Mia, on the other hand, was very intelligent and a star pupil. The comparison between the two of us was almost sad, at least from my vantage point.

In England, I'd garnered the respect of everyone. Sally and I owned that world. Now back in California, I learned quickly I was far from rock-star status. At Marymount in Westwood, I was to be hit much harder by what appeared to me to be an even more sobering reality than what I had faced in grammar school. Just as

I was starting to feel that I had overcome and shed my past creepiness, I was to enter the formidable world of this new high school where beauty was everything.

In this new environment, any ray of hope was utterly shattered within my first month when the senior-class girls, Mia's classmates, chose their "little sisters" from the incoming freshman class. None of Mia's friends, even with bribes, would choose me. In grammar school, I had tried too hard to be one of the crowd and fit in. In the year or so since that time, I realized I would never fit in and gave up trying. This latest reality somehow strangely emancipated me from any care or concern. I lived life with a renewed sense of abandon, becoming wilder and wilder.

My father before his passing, and now Edna, not knowing quite what to do with me, gradually gave up. I did whatever I wanted, whenever I wanted, hanging out with the "fast" crowd. Family and friends watched in horror as my demeanor morphed from child to teenager to overly made-up hoochie with foot-high ratted hair, white-erase lips, eyes hiding behind black mascara and false eyelashes, tight black skirts, a huge bust line padded with soft nylon stockings, and a cigarette dangling from my mouth. When my father was alive, it was much harder for me to smoke my cigarettes and stay out partying late at night. But after his death, although I still had to sneak around Edna, it got much easier.

Edna was good-natured and fun. Her hair was reddish black and stuck straight out from her head with not a curl in it, giving a forked look. She appeared to be of Aboriginal origins, especially when she was angry and yelling. I fondly called her Harpoon! She didn't mind, for she had her vivid images of me as well. She also had a great sense of humor. Edna drove us younger children to our schools and took us wherever we needed to go after school. One day she played a wicked joke on me that she enjoyed so thoroughly I hated her and had to get even.

I was in detention after school for the week, so she had to pick me up later than usual. This particular day the car was packed with brown cardboard boxes. I climbed into the front seat next to her and closed the door. As we drove away, the box piled high in the seat behind me, near my head, had a faint little scratching noise coming from it. She looked at me and asked, "What was that?" I told her I didn't know, that I really hadn't noticed much. The noise came again. She looked at me with horror on her face, repeating in a strong hoarse whisper, "What was that?" Immediately I registered mouse or rat, but before I could say anything, I leaped from the car into the street in fear, forgetting we were in a moving vehicle. She pulled the car to the side, buckled over the steering wheel in hysteria, laughing so hard she could not speak for at least five minutes solid.

I was angry as I watched her doubled over, waiting for her to be able to communicate. Finally, she told Tisa to come out from under the boxes. I screamed at her, telling her she could have killed me. She apologized profusely, but it wasn't very convincing as she held back still more gales of laughter. For days I had to look at that smiling face and repressed hint of laughter in her eyes when she looked at me. Her unabashed amusement in my humiliation had to be matched. And so began a long series of torture poor Harpoon had to endure.

Every night, close to bedtime, we were expected to go upstairs and get ready for bed. Edna, in turn, walked alone through the large empty rooms of our old Spanish-style home, checking each and turning out lights as she left. She hated doing this and was noticeably frightened by it. Every evening I stood behind the dining room drapes wearing a pair of the gardener's shoes sticking out below the drapes. I stayed in the shadows so the quiet dark bulge of a human figure could be seen looming behind. She passed swiftly through the dining area with this haunting dark figure just off to her side view. The first time she saw it, she was frightened to death, but I continued night after night just to unsettle her psyche in preparation for the grand finale.

Edna went from bedroom to bedroom, checking on each of us and saying good night before closing our doors, which we were to lock ourselves from the inside, for she had issued us our own keys. She was so proud of this method of security she had devised. She explained how safe she felt, for even if the house were robbed, the robbers could not enter our locked rooms. I detected a little bit too much pride in her attitude. So the idea came to me to lock my door from the outside, hide in her room, and let her check my locked door. It took a couple days of training so she did not get suspicious. Usually, I argued with her and turned the lights back on after she left. Now I would have the lights out, the door locked, and the covers tucked around me before she had to ask. After several days of this, she made a point of saying how very proud she was of me for such improved behavior.

Finally, when I felt she was ready and there was no chance of suspicion, I waited patiently hunched over behind a chair in a corner of her room. I heard her check my door and yell, "Good girl!" as she had recently taken to doing. She wished me a good night's sleep and then, humming (which she always did) and whistling (which she sometimes did), came contentedly into her room. Feeling safe and secure, she locked her door. I waited until she was in bed, lights out, settled in. Maybe five minutes in, the opportunity presented itself. I was watching how headlights of cars as they passed shone through the light curtains hanging from the street-facing picture window, reflecting on the bed and opposite wall.

I heard a truck coming with a very loud engine. Its lights were brighter than the cars'. By the time it reached the point where its lights came in the window, it was exceptionally bright and very loud. I crawled silently across the room and was now alongside her bed. At that optimum moment, just as the truck's lights flashed across the bed and onto her face, I leaped up, darkening her with my large looming shadow (I had put on a dark overcoat), and grabbed her by the throat. She didn't put up a struggle, not even a scream. Thinking my joke hadn't worked and that I didn't scare her enough, I grabbed her neck harder and shook her more roughly. She was completely limp in my hands. I heard a faint high-pitched sigh of resignation come from her. I realized my joke had worked way too well. She lay limp in my hands for some time. I began shaking her and pulled off my overcoat, yelling at her that it was all a joke. It was me, Prudy. Finally, shaken to her core, she came around. She had always acted like she could handle anything, so I never expected this response. It was horrible, and from that point on, we had a truce never to prank each other again.

After school ended in mid-June, Edna went east with us and stayed for a month helping us settle in at our new home in Connecticut. We stayed on for the next year, attending local schools. My mother, again thinking she had taken the wiser path, thought it best for us to be out of New York City and in the country. So once more we were left to our own devices. Edna found it very difficult to be away from the man she lived with and was homesick all the time. She was like a child in the evenings and, at night, frightened by every little creak or sound generated by the aging house. Many times we had to calm her fears. Often at night we all slept together in the same room.

The house in Connecticut was the former home of Leopold Godowsky Jr., one of the men who developed revolutionary Kodachrome and Technicolor technologies that introduced the color spectrum to cinematography. The house was a very large two-story sprawling building with huge grounds that stretched sixty-three mostly wooded acres. It was an old English manor-style home with a long winding driveway and spacious lawn in front and back. The home was set on a small hill that sloped down to a large pond fed by a rapid stream on one side and spilled over on the other into a small waterfall approximately thirty feet wide and dropping at least twenty feet down into another rockier stream. Behind the pond were a tennis court and small cabin. The woods were terrific for hiking and easy to get lost in. When my mother came, we went for long walks, and as usual, she made it even more beautiful and enchanting than it already was.

thirteen

Uncharted Impermanence

As Johnny, Steffi, Tisa, and I explored the grounds around our new Connecticut home, we made them our own. I inaugurated a huge moss-covered stone by the waterfall as my wishing stone, for it resembled the one I had seen in Ireland. In the winter, we ice-skated on the frozen pond. We looked forward to this with great imagination and fantasy, but when winter finally came the reality hit us. After two hours of clearing away snow, a fifteen-square-foot space was plenty. After the next heavy snow, ice-skating wasn't such a great thing anyway.

When we arrived at our new home that first summer of 1963, the novelty of its setting thrilled us. We met neighbors our age living in the house just downstream. They were as excited to meet us as we were to meet them. We got caught up in one another's excitement. Getting up at sunrise, we stayed out all day exploring, swimming, hiking, and playing. There wasn't enough time for us to do it all. We hardly had time to eat.

There was a canoe for us to use on the pond. We swam like crazy in the rapid river streams, especially the one entering the pond.

It had deep pools that it washed us into, and the rocks were perfectly spaced. We spent hours playing in that area. After about two weeks, as our frantic enthusiasm lost some of its spark, we noticed some rather undesirable creatures in those ponds and streams. It began one afternoon when Steffi stepped into the canoe and let out a scream. We all raced to see a very large ugly spider resting on the oar and another creeping under the canoe's seat board.

Johnny, already in the canoe, tried to jump from it but his heavy foot went partially through the boat's floor, which was canvas of some sort. We inspected our environment more, finding horrid frogs swimming among us and on the shore's edges. Dark shadowy spaces appeared more and more frequently all around the pond. Ugly brown bloated fish swam near the surface, and creatures slithered everywhere along the bottom. To even swim along the edges of the pond, where a sandy bottom shone through, was done only by the most daring of us and only in brief sprints.

One day an investigative party, headed by Jamie, the oldest of our neighbors, went out on the pond in the now-damaged canoe. Johnny bailed water to keep the canoe from filling up. We were investigating a strange growth spotted in the pond near the area where the first stream entered. We went equipped with tools long enough to probe deeply. Jamie hooked a lily-like root vine and began pulling. Suddenly, he pulled up a huge round white jelly-like bulb that was larger than a cantaloupe. It looked like a human brain. We all gasped. He poked it gently and pried it open as it rested in the sun on the flat end of the oar over the water. It was filled with corpuscles and veins, purple and red, with what looked like white fleshy muscle and tissue between. We all screamed with horror. He dropped the oar. The growth disappeared into the dark shadows of the water, and we raced, as fast as we could, back to shore with only one oar.

The next day, a smaller scouting party went out timidly to investigate further. No trace of the jelly mass (nor the oar) was found. Our final consensus was that it was some kind of growth from outer space, a notion probably inspired by some alien movie we'd seen a few years back. We never swam in the pond again, and it was quite a while before we returned anywhere near that area. By the end of two weeks, the whole outdoors was rather undesirable.

We also developed some bad habits. Perhaps it was because of all our fears but, in any case, we avoided sleep, staying up through the night, watching *The Steve Allen Show*. Gradually, our extended evenings included not just the late show, but also the late, late show. As a result, we slept in until three or four in the afternoon and, by the end of the summer, we didn't even bother to dress except to occasionally change our pajamas or nightgowns. Our interest in the delights and activities of daylight dwindled to a minimum. Our new guardian, Sue Hahn, didn't seem to care as long as we didn't cause any trouble.

Sue was our cook and caretaker. She had short gray hair, which she kept in a hairnet. She was happy to work this job because my mother promised her the brand-new blue Buick she was driving if she stayed a year. She was obviously beside herself to have this new car and came alive whenever she spoke of it. Her eyes twinkled and lit up like a child's. Sometimes she took us for a spin just so she could drive it. She kept the seats, dashboard, and steering wheel covered in vinyl.

After about a month, Sue let it slip one night at dinner that her real name was Minnie Sue. Johnny, Steffi, Tisa, and I laughed, but not to be mean. Maybe I missed something, for Sue became extremely defensive, like a child. So, as if smelling blood, we all chanted, "Minnie Sue, Minnie Sue." She said loudly and slowly, her voice controlled and calm, that she did not wish to be called Minnie Sue. Something about an adult begging a kid to behave can only bring out the worst. We laughed and said we would call her Minnie Sue from now on. It was a cute name, nothing to be ashamed of. Slamming her silverware on the table, she got up, stormed out, and declared she was not coming out of her room the rest of the evening. We would have to do our own dishes and clean up. Of course, no one did.

Everyone was a little startled by her extreme reaction; it was unexpected and got out of control so fast. The next day at dinner, Johnny called her Minnie Sue again. She walked out once more and pouted around the kitchen for several days. In her first month, Sue had begun her job with care and enthusiasm. It was sad to watch this deteriorate so quickly.

Within a week of the Minnie Sue incident, she made us a lovely chocolate cake from scratch and hid it in the bread box. It was for Tisa's birthday. She worked hard on the cake, decorating it herself, and wouldn't let us in the kitchen. There was an air of excitement. Finally, it was done and cooling.

At dinner, Sue slipped out early, motioning excitedly for Steffi and me to come help light the candles. Suddenly a loud gasp from the kitchen was followed by violent screaming: "Who did this? Who did this? Who is so wicked to do this?" Silence. Sue's face turned white with pink blotches scattered across it. She shook with fury. As she entered the dining room and faced the table where we all sat, she broke, becoming almost meek. "Who would do such a terrible thing?" Her voice was small now. She tore off her apron, throwing it on the floor. "I don't believe you people." Storming into her room, she slammed and locked the door behind her and was not seen for what seemed like a couple of days. Patrick, aged 20, visiting for the weekend, had done it. Thinking it funny, he put his hand right in the middle of the top of the cake, leaving a big handprint across it. He had also cut a piece and eaten it.

When we saw Sue again, she was very cold and awkward, not knowing how to treat us. It was a long time before she relaxed around us, and even then she never let her guard down. The friendly merriment she had once shown us, spilling over with childlike enthusiasm, was gone in just over a month. No more stories told with twinkling eyes, bubbling personality.

A part of Sue we did not miss, which was both annoying and endearing, was her amazing ability to continuously use the word "hun," short for honey. She managed to stick it on the end of every sentence. One evening, we counted them. She said "hun" at least twenty times during the course of one meal. "Pass the butter, hun." "Thank you, hun." "Do you want some more buns, hun?" "What, hun?" "Don't knock your glass, hun."

But singsongy Sue was now solemn Sue, cautious Sue. She was Sue who didn't trust or like us. Resigned, Sue was seen less and less as the year wore on. She lived in her room with the television on, and rarely interacted with us. She left our food on the table and rang a bell. We were stunned to see the change in her because it happened so abruptly. It was disturbing when we realized the old happy friendly Sue would never come back, that our damage was irreparable.

In the fall, I attended the local public high school. Twenty-five hundred students were enrolled, and it was like a zoo. I had never seen anything like it. There were four academic levels—A, B, C, D—based on students' test scores. I raced through the test, randomly filling in empty boxes. I figured if I got a low score, I would be put in easy classes and wouldn't have to work at all. I also had a hint of worry that, even if I tried, I might end up in the lower classes anyway, so why humiliate myself?

I was placed in level C. I spoke with the guidance counselor, who said if I wasn't interested in going to college, I could take classes such as typing, homemaking, art, sewing, home economics, and general math. I needed to meet only a certain number of units to graduate. I thought I had it made. I'd never have to do homework. My future and college were a million years away. Who knew what would happen between now and then? I could be dead. There could be a war. The world could end.

We briefly saw Sue for a few minutes daily when she took us in her prized blue Buick to the bus stop just down the street. The trips to school on the school bus were short-lived. In late September Johnny got his driver's license and a 1958 white Porsche convertible. I would ride with him daily to school. The school had so many kids filling the hallways, voices echoing loudly. It was my first exposure to a large institutional environment, impersonal and empty. It scared and depressed me, but I was also intrigued by the newness of it.

Coinciding with the academic chain, the high school's social structure was also four-tiered:

1. Creeps, now commonly referred to as nerds, were often the studious ones in level A.

2. High Y's (standing for YMCA), today called jocks, were usually all-American football types. Their parents were mostly businessmen who commuted to work on trains into New York. Their mothers typically drank and took a lot of prescription drugs. They were level B.
3. Beatniks—which in today's culture might include the goths, hippies, and artsy types—also filled level B. They were pre-hippie, artistic, with long hair, turtlenecks, and corduroy pants, and often into recreational drug use.
4. Greasers (and I) filled levels C and D classes. These were rougher kids who didn't want to be there, more like our present-day urban gang types. They were usually from poorer working-class backgrounds and predominantly Irish, Italian, Puerto Rican, or black. The boys wore greased pompadour hairdos, tight pants, and pointed shoes. The girls had ratted hair and tight skirts, chewed gum, and swore a lot.

I found it fascinating to be in level C with these students. They misbehaved far more than anyone I'd ever known. They were outrageous. They were violent. They were crude. They were loud and never took a class seriously. There was always terrific humor and high comedy as the students talked back to teachers. Their wonderfully clever cracks could set the entire class off for as long as five solid minutes of wild laughter and whistling. Classes mostly consisted of running comments between students. Fights broke out. It was impossible to listen to the teacher and far more interesting to be involved in the students' antics.

At first I entered these classes wide-eyed and naive. The girls called me "cute," but as time went on and I began listening more carefully to the running dialogues, I realized the students were colorful and amusing but that some were also extremely dangerous. They were always sweet to me, but among one another they were street-tough. The girls carried switchblades in their hair. One morning, a rather fat Italian girl came to school all cut up. She had been in a "cat fight" with a black girl I liked who was very outspoken and extremely amusing. She provoked the Italian girl over something to do with a boyfriend, and they fought after school in the yard. These two were so tough that even the boys didn't go near them.

Their fight was very serious because eventually many kids from their two cliques were brought into it. The Italian girl had been hurt quite badly. The next day the rival groups provoked one another in classes. There were sudden outbursts of violence, with boys flashing switchblades. At the end of that day, a violent encounter between the gangs continued into the night. Many kids missed classes for a couple days, and the next few weeks were very dangerous. Kids were thrown right out of class for violent behavior, and many were suspended or expelled.

My attention at this time was focused on the beatnik group of kids. They seemed so much more interesting than the others. They loved good music, art, and philosophy, and I learned a lot about these disciplines from them. But overall, they were self-destructive, spoiled, and using way too many drugs. Nonetheless, I was infatuated and aspired to be one of them. Some older ones occasionally joined those of us still in high school. There was a very charismatic guy named Kenny, who was into heroin. At twenty or twenty-one, he was not a student but a lingerer. His friends, who came in from the city, were all heavy addicts and our area drug dealers.

Kenny was the real McCoy, and I found myself enticed by him. One of his dealer friends, a black guy, sort of short, had a most likeable smile. Another, a very tall white guy with a deep cutting voice like an actor, was an obvious good-looker, but up close his face had no character nor did his personality. Another of his friends looked liked James Dean in his motorcycle era, with a very delinquent manner, a bad boy for sure but funny with a lot of energy. His name was Jeff. These were seriously troubled people I was running with now. All were in their mid- to late twenties. Kenny was truly a tragic character. He overdosed at a party and nearly died, but his friend got him in the bathtub and revived him. Everyone really liked him. And he was outright killing himself. This was heartbreaking. He shot himself in the head a year later. The delinquent one, Jeff, OD'd shortly after, and so did Jeff's girlfriend.

I hung around these guys, with ugly fearful fascination, watching them shoot up. I was just beginning to experiment with illegal substances, but I drew the line at heroin. I would never shoot it into my bloodstream no matter how bad I got. To me, it was the worst thing next to suicide. So I watched, enthralled with a perverse horror. It was as if they had sold their souls to the devil. Once having taken it, few seemed to ever get completely out of its clutches.

I also spent time with the younger set of beats from school. These were bad kids, too, but younger and more innocent. They were heading down the same path, but there was still hope since they had other interests besides drugs, like being involved in music, art, philosophy, and religion. My brother Johnny and some of his new friends from school cut a deal with an old drunkard, who bought alcohol for us if we paid him. So we had alcohol flowing.

On New Year's Eve, at the end of 1963, I went to a party with the beatniks from school. I was drunk and full of alcohol-induced personality and confidence. I was talking to just the person I wanted to talk to, but alongside him was another fellow who wanted to talk to me. I could feel this, but I wasn't interested. I was attracted to the most superficially flashy beatnik-looking dude, and next to him was this other very laid-back but intense presence who was clearly interested in me. The beatnik I wanted to talk to was not particularly bright and didn't have much to say. He was young and immature. It was a letdown, but he looked the part so well that I was still interested.

The one next to him annoyed me because it seemed I was going to have to talk with him whether I liked it or not. His name was Tom, and he became my boyfriend for the next year and a half. Tom was nineteen, very interesting and sensitive. His older brother was a heroin addict and extremely screwed up. Tom lived in fear of ending up like him. He was very fear-ridden and barely coping with life. He was the oldest and most revered by all the beatnik kids in school. He stayed quiet for long periods of time, and the other kids all thought he was so wise.

Everyone in this group was mostly into music and painting. Tom had no talents and was really a thinker. He loved wisdom, wherever it was to be found. He introduced me to a lot of Eastern, Indian, and Buddhist thought. He loved Henry Miller. I didn't appreciate Tom at first, thinking that if he thought I was so great he couldn't be too neat himself. But his sadness and depth quietly won me over, and we became very close.

I was on the precipice of the most destructive period of my life. I dove in head first, giving myself over to my newly adopted rationale that we only live once. I would have probably moved into this period earlier, but it was not until the New Year's party that I finally had a bunch of good friends who were heading downhill with me. At the party, I became an established part of the crowd because Tom, whom they all admired, had openly expressed his liking for me. The girls wanted to be my friend, and the boys immediately liked me. I also met one other person of importance. I'd noticed her before at school, and her name was Mara. She approached me at the party, asking about my brother Johnny. She would play a role later in my Manhattan life.

At the same time Tom came into my life, another boy, Andy, also was attracted to me. The New Year's party was a mixture of two different crowds: the beatniks and high Y's. Andy, like Tom, was older and greatly respected by his fellow peers in the high-Y crowd. I was not in the least interested in Andy but greatly flattered by his crush on me. At this party, he said he and I had been making eye contact during lunch for months and that he had tried approaching me. But I always looked past him or had been unfriendly. He was so glad we were finally meeting this evening. The truth was that I had never seen him before because I only wore my eyeglasses in class. I was very nearsighted.

Once the party ended and school resumed after holiday break, I began hanging out regularly with my newfound friends. The problem for me was that I did not have the gregarious personality my school friends expected after meeting me at the party. They only knew the drunken me, the party me. Now I was sober and so shy. Tom kept asking if I was ill. "Do you feel well?"

I wanted so badly to be friends with these people. It meant so much to me, but how could they want to be my friends? I was that

creep, the ugly girl no one liked. I was petrified that I might lose
them all, the boys and girls. Surely they wouldn't put up with much
more of this quiet unsure dowdy person who never had anything
to say. I became panicky; my time was running out. So I began
drinking on the sly. The fun-lover was back, the party person they
knew. I could deal with the crowd again, and *everything* we did was
done in a group. We drove around in a group. We hung out on
Saturday nights and lazy afternoons, always in a group. Together
in a group we played and listened to music, got high on pot, and
even sniffed glue.

I was a real boon to the group because of the big house I lived in
with relatively little supervision, lots of property, no nearby houses
and, most important, no parents. Our large house very quickly
became the hangout. No more cruising around in cars. Everyone
came to my place. There was a large room in the basement, which
Sue let us use. As long as we were not noisy and rowdy, she felt
we were behaving well. We didn't get rambunctious with pot, and
our music was not loud. So we had the run of the place, while Sue
stayed in her room watching TV or napping. We rarely worried
about her since she made it clear she didn't care what we did as
long as we didn't bother her. The large basement room was off to
the side of the house, completely separate. We called it the Purple
Room because it was all done in purple, from the rugs to the curtains and upholstery, and even purple-flowered wallpaper.

Now that we had a safe place to hang out, all we ever did was
get high by some means or another. It became my lifestyle. Since it
was my place, it wasn't just an occasional afternoon or evening—it
was daily and nightly. On weekends, Sue futilely tried to stop the
invasion, which continued to grow as word spread. People raided
the refrigerator and freezer, cooking meals at all hours and mess-
ing up the kitchen. Nothing ever got cleaned up, and things were
stolen. Sue had to step in, in spite of herself, but her words were
empty. No one listened. She was humored, but nothing she said
was heeded. Eventually, she just locked herself safely in her room.

The older junkie friends moved in and lived at the house.
The two groups mixed, and I was sad to see some of the results.

Huge parties developed every Friday and Saturday night. Word had spread far and wide, way past our local town. People were told about a house with no parents, where parties were continuous. The police circled the area like sharks, but they rarely got a catch. As long as we kept under six or nine cars, something like that, they could not raid the house. Some kids stepped in and orchestrated car pools and shuttle services. Liquor was no problem since the junkies were old enough to buy it.

I regularly drank muscatel, because it was so cheap. Apparently it had ether in it. I went whole evenings not remembering what I did. By about April, I was going to school high, drinking there, and then coming home drunk. I learned I could sell liquor at exorbitant prices. One night I sold Johnny's stash, and he caught me. In a drunken stupor, fearing he would kill me, I hit him over the head with a bottle, knocking him out and cutting his face. Blood was everywhere. I had for months been getting progressively more out of hand and violently so. I was shocked by what I had done to Johnny and sat stunned as he was rushed to the hospital. Quickly, the whole place cleared out. Luckily he was not hurt badly, but I could have blinded him or worse.

I was becoming untrustworthy and immoral. I hated myself. I lied all the time, even when I didn't need to. I cheated those around me, for instance, selling Johnny's liquor at large profits for myself. I watered it down and sold two for one. As I sat miserably on the staircase, I looked down. Blood was gushing from my right hand. I was horrified but at the same time elated. I didn't know how I would face Johnny and everyone else. As it turned out, I was hurt worse than he was, a long sheath of glass lodged between my thumb and fingers. It had cut a tendon. I paid a heavy price at the hospital because I could not be sedated due to the alcohol and had to remain awake during the whole procedure while they sewed the tendon.

It was awful for me and just as bad for the hospital staff. I was completely unruly, screaming, swearing, yelling, and talking back. Jumping up every few seconds, I had to be held down by quite a few orderlies. Because I was so drunk, most of it was a blur. I was completely obnoxious, fighting with everyone. I didn't even remember doing some of the horrible things I heard about the next day.

The parties at our house were becoming less desirable to others. Eventually only the hard-core partiers were there on the weekends, and even that crowd thinned. I was the only noisy and loud one, for everyone in our group was moving away from alcohol and into drugs. One quiet night, I provoked a dangerous physical fight with one of the girls. There was hitting, hair pulling, biting, and scratching. My opponent was very cool to me after that incident, but I remained friendly since I had no recollection of it.

A week or so after my tendon was cut, we had another big weekend bash. Drinks were flowing, and I was in my obnoxious prime, thinking I was the cutest creature on earth and flirting with everyone. I drank some white wine, among many other things. I remember this particular wine because it had mold or film covering it. I didn't care. I was drunk, and I downed it.

The next morning I woke up completely swollen beyond recognition. It was amazing. My fingers were so large they were completely compressed into one hideous large flat fat block of flesh. I was unable to bend them at all. My feet were huge, toes also smashed together. It seemed they should burst. It was quite a sight. All the others hanging out in our home, including Kenny, came to my bedroom and peered in, fascinated by this sight reminiscent of *Creature from the Black Lagoon*. Most of these friends tried not to laugh, for I was in such pain. Sue took good care of me during this time.

I itched and ached intensely for about a week or so, and Sue was wonderful and adoring. I was particularly surprised by her compassion. She took such good care of me, always trying to lessen my pain. Her genuine kindness touched me very deeply. And while I was completely at her mercy, she never ceased to pour as much wisdom as she could on me. I'm sure she was hoping something would penetrate and that, when I regained my health, she would no longer be faced with the party monster. She raced back and forth between the bathroom and bedroom with hot tea compresses. Gently covering me with the compresses, she told me tannic acid in the tea reduces swelling and itching.

I lay in bed in such pain for hours, only able to look upward at the ceiling for my neck was swollen so thick it could not be bent or turned. Sue bustled busily about me, cheerfully humming church hymns just under her breath, while I watched from the corners of my eyes. I knew she didn't have to go to all this trouble for me. I so appreciated and enjoyed her gentle manner as she untiringly changed one compress after another. The doctor gave me ointment, which didn't work nearly as well as Sue's tea and tannic acid. I loved her for her care, and we developed a tight rapport during that time. She stayed with me late at night, talking gaily, telling me stories from her past to distract me from the pain.

And always as she leaned over to change another compress, she drove home her wisdom: "This is God's will, hun. He's trying to teach you a lesson. You're a lucky girl. The angels are looking after you and care enough to spank you."

In the back of my mind, I agreed with her. I *was* lucky. However brief, for those few days, I reflected on deeper issues and had moments remembering God, but I was mired too deeply in my own muck. After this experience, I was terrified to drink again. The doctor said I had developed an allergy to alcohol, causing hives, and it could happen again. I stayed far away from alcohol after that, but unfortunately there were other ways to lose myself, such as abuse of marijuana, amphetamines, and many other toxic substances…and I still had a lot to learn.

JOHNNY, PRUDENCE, STEFFI AND TISA IN THE IRELAND 1959

WATERFALL FLOWING FROM
THE POND ON THE WESTPORT
PROPERTY

MODELING PICTURE OF PRUDENCE
IN NYC 1965

fourteen

Continuation: Delving Deeper

In the middle of all the chaos my life had become, I was getting to know Tom better. He was a quiet soul, very sensitive. Although he was self-destructive in the way we all were, he also had sophisticated aesthetic sensibilities. He loved genuine art, diverse and excellent music, and intelligent and perceptive thinking. He was not particularly knowledgeable on these subjects but approached them as a student of life, asking himself how they made him feel, how they refined his senses, elevating to more spiritual and expansive emotions. Tom approached everyone and everything mindful of this goal, which was foremost in everything he did even if sometimes misguided. Because he had been crushed by his life, he was fear-ridden and negative about himself. Nonetheless, he guided me toward what is right and just in life, no matter how deep we got in the mire.

He inspired me to read Hermann Hesse's classic *Siddhartha*, about one man's spiritual journey during the time of Buddha. The book uses Buddhist principles, combined with the basic philosophy of the *Upanishads* and *Bhagavad Gita* scriptures. Its fundamental message is that unity underlies and pervades everything. We can only find lasting peace by connecting with that oneness or wholeness deep within through meditation.

This was my first exposure to Eastern thought, and I perceived it as revolutionary. Its basis is the most beautiful, simple, universal, and profound philosophy of life I had ever heard: The essence of the human soul, deep within each of us, is divine. I thought of this as so sublime in its perfection. This is why we are human, and nothing is more important. I felt the tug of desire to devote my life to this simple but profound goal, living connected to my inner divine essence. But I was so far from that, restless, unhappy, and lost.

My confused personal sense of life and living was playing out against the backdrop of increasingly turbulent political and social times. President John F. Kennedy was shot months earlier, in November 1963, his brutal murder aired on television worldwide. A life, which had inspired hope for so many, was senselessly taken. As a nation, we mourned collectively in disbelief and shock. Glued to our television sets, we watched the horrific drama unravel as Lee Harvey Oswald was caught and then murdered before our eyes by nightclub owner Jack Ruby. And so began the unraveling of positive expectation for many of us in the coming generation.

Still deeply ensconced in my own quagmire, and very lost, I continued sinking deeper. I went to school stoned almost every day. I got away with not doing schoolwork, but I still had to attend school. Sue, under a renewed directive from my mother, was very strict and watched me with an eagle's eye. This made it practically impossible to cut classes. As the school year progressed and spring was well under way, a group of us regularly met after school to get high. Now that I could no longer drink because of my allergic reaction, I was quite content with Dexedrine and codeine. A girl friend had a refillable codeine supply prescribed for premenstrual symptoms, and another couple of girls had diet-pill prescriptions.

With the constant parties and wild antics, it was no huge surprise we'd nabbed the attention of authorities. In late spring 1964, police notified my mother that we could no longer remain in Connecticut unattended. She would have to take us to Manhattan at the end of the school year. Sue had given up on me—we were barely on speaking terms by the time she left in June. She returned to Michigan and her former work as a mortician's beautician, which I imagine was very appealing after a year with us. She had served her time. Finishing her required year meant she finally owned her cherished blue Buick. I never saw her again.

Even though we moved to Manhattan, I continued hanging out with my friends, whether in Connecticut or New York, in our self-indulgent ways. We acted spoiled, lazy, slothful, selfish, self-centered, and, most of all, disrespectful of life. The only way out of our deplorable state of being, as far as we knew, was to get higher or try different types of highs. Unhappy with myself and irreverent toward life and all I had been given, I felt hollow, constipated, and stale inside. I was abusing myself, and nothing could relieve the feeling of emptiness. I couldn't conceive of how I could continue like this. My days felt haunted, weighing on me a heavy air of premonition of what was looming.

That summer, one of our friend's parents went out of town and left him alone in his house. This meant the whole group had a place to live and get high for two weeks. As long as I notified my mother where I was staying (she never checked), I had the freedom to go anywhere and be anywhere. Tom and a friend mailed away to Texas for peyote, and after about three weeks received in the mail some large heavy boxes packed tightly to the top with numerous peyote buttons. None of us were sure what to expect from a peyote high. We only knew Native Americans used peyote in their sacred rituals and that it was a hallucinogenic, whatever that meant. Well, we were about to find out.

The peyote high turned out to be amazing, familiar, totally spiritual. It was very similar to the experience I'd had earlier, after my father's death, in the little desert cabin outside Los Angeles. I was awed by and felt safe with peyote. It reinforced what was most important to me—the quest for spirituality and truth. It was clear I was dealing with something very sacred, that I could not manipulate or abuse. It was not just a quick buzz I could cop whenever I wanted.

The experience—even though, or rather *because*, it was so awe-inspiring—left me once again disoriented in my life. Remembering my spiritual roots, I renewed my desire to devote myself to God. But how? I was so deeply immersed in my own morass I couldn't begin to find my way out. I was reminded, now more than ever, of a higher power, so quietly in my mind I pleaded for help.

Later that summer of 1964, at the Newport Folk Festival in Rhode Island, I took peyote again. I had the vivid experience of being asked, mentally, if I wanted to serve a higher purpose. I was communicating with a superior being or intelligence. My response was of complete submission, subservience even. I would obey without hesitation. There was no sense of fear, no room for that. When I was asked if I wanted to serve, I was also told I would have to suffer a tremendous amount. I agreed to serve. Immediately, I was thrown into a very paranoid frame of mind.

The telepathic exchange, while not vocal, seemed to be with two higher beings. Their conversation with me was not very clear at the time, because I kept switching from my ordinary reality to this other dimension. Gradually over time, it became clearer to me what they had asked, as I relived the experience over and over in my mind. I am aware this could very well have been my imagination, under the influence of a hallucinogen, playing tricks on me. Nonetheless, it instilled in me hope that I might be able to turn my life around.

At the show in Newport, Bob Dylan, Joan Baez, Dave Van Ronk, Pete Seeger, and many other voices sang and spoke for peace and change. It was a quiet rebellion. I heard about peaceful resistance for the first time, how we could say no nonviolently. I returned to a different kind of folk festival the next year, in 1965, with the immediacy of the Vietnam War and military draft dictating and dominating conversations. Rather than a gentle awakening, the discourse was now a boldly imperative call for action to stop senseless violence and bloodshed in an unnecessary war. A public tsunami was brewing, fueled by increasing despondency among my peers, many of whom were drafted for what appeared to be a remote and obscure war. Widespread introduction of recreational psychedelic drug use contributed to the stormy scene.

In the fall of 1964, I was sent to a Vermont boarding school carefully chosen by a psychiatrist my mother had hired to treat me. She felt certain the school would positively influence me, as it was known for taking difficult children. My mother finally breathed a sigh of relief and left to tour with her Broadway show, feeling confident I was safely out of temptation's way. I lasted one week, a record for me.

I was completely unruly and disobedient. After having my own schedule for so long, coming and going freely, I didn't even understand rules or how to follow them. I was so used to doing whatever I wanted whenever I wanted, without reporting to anyone, that I often forgot and wandered off, never alerting anyone or asking permission. I meant no malice. My intention was to do the right thing, but when a bunch of my Connecticut friends unexpectedly descended on the school to visit me, I spent the night camping out with them before remembering to ask permission. This was the final straw.

I wanted so badly to start afresh, but old habits and karmas got in the way. I returned to New York more despondent than ever. My mother's show was closing on Broadway, and she and her cast were spending a full year on the road, touring nationally. The four of us younger kids—Johnny, Steffi, Tisa, and I—were once again left with no parental guidance, only this time in Manhattan! To be fair to my mother, she was distraught that I was sent home. I was given the back washroom in the hall behind our apartment as my room. It had a large deep sink for washing laundry that dominated the small space, and many of the sputtering and gushing pipes that ran overhead and along the walls channeled the apartment's plumbing. My mother tried to make it cheerful by adding a thick red carpet and painting the high ceiling sky blue.

I decided this might be my chance to really pull myself together. Our New York apartment was on the Upper West Side, overlooking Central Park. It was a beautiful old high-rise, next to the famous Dakota building, where John Lennon later lived…and died, at its entrance. Basil Rathbone, most famous for playing Sherlock Holmes in many films, resided in the apartment across the hall from us. Now considered an upscale area, during this period in the mid-'60s, the Upper West Side was very dangerous and impoverished. Sherman Square, nicknamed Needle Park for its frequent loitering by intravenous drug users, was just down the street. We never left the apartment at night, for fear of being robbed or stabbed.

We four kids were mostly cared for by a beautiful black woman, Constance from Barbados. She was young, only twenty-four, and loved to hang out with us, our boyfriends, and our drugs. She developed a crush on my boyfriend Tom and took a strong disliking to me. She lived with us a year, sleeping in my mother's bedroom, cooking meals, and managing household chores. Johnny, Steffi, and Tisa continued to go to school and live semi-normal lives. My mother enrolled me in a private New York school called Staples High School upon my return. Unfortunately I did not last there very long either.

My makeshift room was so small that there was barely enough space for a single bed. On the back wall, up toward the high ceiling, was a small window overlooking the backs of many buildings. This little window and its view of New York City's underbelly was almost a life form of its own, bustling and busy, standing in sharp contrast to the barren walls and clanging pipes of my drab cold sterile little washroom. I loved and hated peering out that window and spent many hours at it. I was on the eleventh floor; most other buildings sprawled below me. The view from the window captivated me with its dreariness, stretching in all directions. It showcased filthy dirty stained brick structures of varying shapes and sizes, some with laundry hanging out, others with smoke coming from their smokestacks. At night, the drab little world below lit up, thousands of little windows brightly shining in the dark night until the ugly world below glistened like a million jewels set against the blackened sky.

That year in that room was the most depressing time of my life. Again, I was on my own, with no one seeming to care what I did. Most of my friends in New York and Connecticut smoked a lot of pot, but they continued to go to school and keep up a front of normalcy. I tried charting a new course, but I was quickly demoralized as I confronted a new school and a schedule, which I had no idea how to follow as I had never really done homework. Over time I stopped going to school and stayed isolated in my room.

The washroom sink served several necessary functions, so I rarely had to leave. I chain-smoked pot, and the only people I saw were Tom and the girl named Mara who liked my brother Johnny. Both Johnny and I found her interesting and, by the end of the summer, we were good friends with her. Tom and Mara came in from Connecticut to stay weekends with me in my dreary little room. The walls, white-painted concrete, allowed just enough room for my bed and enough floor space for someone to stretch out lengthwise, halfway under the sink, between the bed and wall. This is where Mara slept, while Tom and I shared the bed.

Mara was my closest friend at the time and very influential in my life. Her family had a history of mental illness, and her younger sister, who had dated Johnny for a while, had gone completely mad. Mara herself was always struggling with it and was institutionalized periodically. We poured our thoughts and dreams out to each other, hers always dark, fearful, and very warped. We got high together, swapping concepts and ideas. She always dwelled in the past, remembering it longingly.

I was always delving ever deeper into my psyche, to darker and darker regions, questioning and contemplating. It was very risky, probing so deeply under the influence of excessive drugs. We gradually broke our bonds with the present. She and I hated the present, each for our own reasons. Our sicknesses fed off each other, while drug use further warped and demented us.

When I first moved into the apartment, I often sat in my little washroom-turned-bedroom, smoked a few tokes from my homemade water pipe, closed my eyes, and perceived the most astounding wisdom rambling gently through my mind. It was beautiful and very profound. I grabbed at it as best I could, excited by such serene thoughts. I wrote down what I could to show Mara. We developed a ritual of this, and she was as fascinated by it as I was.

I became more intrigued, but the wisdom came less. My logic was that if the mind could emit such beautiful thoughts, I should go deeper into the mind, to where the thoughts were coming from, for this could only be good. I must trust it and give myself over to it. It felt like a pied piper was leading me toward something very valuable and important. I didn't realize it was luring me toward death.

I listened to my thoughts indiscriminately. The transition started very definitively one evening as I sat in my little room with a couple of New York friends I had met while in school. We were listening to music and getting high, and I was watching everybody. I heard and observed my thoughts, very naturally sizing them up. At first the thoughts were innocent, but then they became loud with a particular sense of pride, judging the others. I felt separated and alone with this interior observer. No longer were my thoughts fleeting and random. A vain petty ugly voice boomed within me, and I could not turn it off.

It was "I." *I* was sitting in judgment of the others. *I* was the voice. And who was I? Who is vanity? Who is pride? Based on my Catholic upbringing, guess who I became? I envied the others' innocence, and I truly feared I was the devil. This living nightmare, which got far worse before it got better, became a battle for my life.

I rarely saw my brother and sisters, except for an occasional party at the apartment. No one, including Constance, seemed to notice. The lonely days between Mara and Tom's weekend visits were hellish and unbearable. For brief moments I felt spurts of joy and life, wanting to go for a walk in the park or maybe visit someone. But after a few minutes, I grew weary and bored with such ideas.

These healthy outbursts dwindled down to merely thinking about getting off the bed or going over to the window or looking out the door. Once in a great while, I imagined going to the living room to talk with my siblings or Constance, but the urge was gone before I ever acted on it. Whenever I thought I might be able to go to the kitchen and get something to eat, I grew fatigued. Having just *considered* all that effort was enough. And so I sat or lay in bed, having only the energy to continue to get high.

fifteen

Continuation: Walking the Precipice

As much as I previously enjoyed their visits, in my depressed state I dreaded weekends when I had to see Tom and Mara. Luckily they rarely wanted to do anything but get high. Once in a while, we went to Mara's cousin's apartment just a couple short blocks away. Once there, I could not conceive of walking back to our apartment and usually took a cab. At home, I saw my siblings heat up meals and wash their dishes. It blew my mind. How did they do that? They were like supermen, for they constantly got high but managed to still function.

Constance hated me beyond belief. She saw me as a white person with every opportunity, throwing away a privileged life. People from where she came worked hard all their lives to have half of what I had. She hated fixing my meals and waiting on me. I was a healthy young woman who should be taking care of herself. I came out of my hole-in-the-wall room only to be hit with a barrage of verbal abuse. Her rage boiled and spewed; blood vessels in her neck popping as she screamed. She let loose her hatred, her eyes flared and bulging. Once, while yelling that she wanted to destroy me with all her heart, she stopped abruptly and in a frighteningly deep voice, a low kind of chant, like a deeply intentional prayer, verbally wished for my destruction.

I didn't understand why she hated me so much, but it was way past any understanding anyway. She calmed down and tolerated me only when Tom was around. At those times, she acted seductively, often putting her arm around him, cajoling him, charming him, and teasing him coyly. She drank and partied with us, but even then, she always let me know she hated me.

One day as I came schlepping out of my room, I was met with a barrage of insults from Constance. We were in the living room when she turned on me in fury, like a wild animal. She grabbed me and brought her face within a half-inch of mine as our eyes met, hers on fire! She screamed, "I curse you and all that you are! *You are the devil!*" Even now it scares me. "May evil befall you," she hissed, along with a few more well-phrased damnations. They were horrifying, with wild voodoo undertones. She was from Barbados and believed in certain things. It frightened me to the core of my being, filling my heart with a terror and fear I would not soon shake.

I was profoundly disturbed by that experience. She had meant it with everything she had. Mara and Tom witnessed it and were extremely shocked by her vehemence. None of us had ever seen anything like it. It seemed to come out of nowhere, filled with the energy of a primitive animal tearing me to shreds. It obviously had been smoldering in her for a long time. After that incident, her hatred was as strong as ever but not as passionate. She knew she had injured me, and perhaps that cooled her down. For me, in my sick world, it only sent me reeling further on my destructive path.

I continued to spend long stretches of time without seeing anyone or coming out of my room. I was tired of Mara and Tom, who took a turn for the worse. He was using heroin seriously and steadily. Seeing this hurt me very much. I saw it on some level as a slight—he chose heroin over me. I couldn't compete with it. He was shooting it regularly, hooked and committed. I hated him. He was starting to see sexually the friend with whom he had once had a homosexual relationship. His homosexuality with this guy bothered him immensely. He wanted my help, but I saw him as weak and wanted nothing to do with him.

Mara and I were still friends, but we were feeding off each other's sickness. She began coming less frequently, actually afraid of being around me as my thoughts grew increasingly darker and more twisted. I stayed in my room growing more intimately familiar with my paranoiac illnesses. I took all my fears from deep inside and, believing them, made them real, lived them out. I suffered severe depression, and this was a new twist for me. Up to that point, I had just dabbled in mental illness, but now I was major league. Mara, too, suffered from bouts of depression for weeks at a time. The illness, so complete in its pain, entirely consumes the psyche. Hope, the natural healthy state of the mind, is temporarily lost.

Mara, finally seeing me as a fellow sufferer, took perverse pleasure in guiding me after having been alone in her own depression for so long. She understood every little quirk, offering no solution but solace in a misery-loves-company sort of way, enabling me to descend deeper. Rather than heeding danger warnings at red-flag points, I had a sympathetic commiserator, a guide who already knew many of the routes. But I was traveling too fast even for her. She got scared, knowing only too well from her experiences and those of her younger sister the terrible price mental illness exacts. For me it was still new, and I had no idea the extent of the toll I was taking on myself. Mara broke off the friendship, and I was too self-involved to care.

I saw her years later, and she was still fighting mental illness. She was heavily sedated, having just come out of a long bout in a mental hospital. Her mannerisms and expressions were the same as they had been when she got high, quick gestures of her hand to her mouth, eyes darting and then opening wide.

We had delved into exploring the nature of reality, from such confused positions of self-hatred and feelings of failure. It was dubious as to whether she or I would make it and be able to sustain a functioning life. This exacerbated the depression and fear.

Still, for most of the year, I didn't realize what I was doing to myself, how far I had fallen. The turning point occurred in my little room just before Easter. I suspect it was evening, because I slept during the day. I had not been out of my room for weeks. I was in the drugged delirium between sleeping and waking, lingering in a state of detachment from full consciousness. Suddenly, sounds that were real—fading footsteps in the hallway, incessant clinking and scraping of elevator chains, banging pipes overhead, car horns, airplanes, and general traffic—seemed dream-like, as if echoing or ricocheting off something.

I was hallucinating but had not taken anything, and I was not high. This frightened me, with good reason. It was not like the experiences I had with peyote—those were not necessarily tangible but very *real*. This was very *unreal*, surrealistic. My physical senses were acutely attuned, and my emotions were at a peak. I was wide awake. Everything was intensified—my perception, colors in the room, sounds, movements. I sat, facing the wall, on my red carpet. From just below the pipes came an undeniable creaking noise—growing louder. I moved closer to examine and saw a clean line along the wall, a crack, arch-shaped, about two feet high. The sound got sharper, and a vague light emitted from behind the crack. The arched section vibrated as the crack widened. It was a door, an opening.

I felt as if I had known all along this door was there and what was behind it. The door opened slowly, interminably, and suddenly in a flash, it crashed open against the wall. Before I had time to register shock or surprise, a peculiar little man popped out. He was strangely alluring but also hideously grotesque. He looked like the man in the French puppet versions of *Punch and Judy*. His face was rubbery, his features large and ugly. His body was dwarfed by a large head and oversize nose. He was about a foot high. His torso was fat, and his arms and legs too short, awkwardly disproportionate. His clothes and grooming were pristine and elegant. I was mesmerized, charmed, and repulsed, all at the same time.

I sensed that I knew him, yet I had never seen him before. He was part of me, a bizarre fragment of my personality projecting from my mind. His facial features moved, and he spoke to me. His mouth opened, but I only heard him telepathically. Everything outside of me was inside my mind, the outside of me and inside of me all the same. His voice bounced through the air like an echo. I watched the whole drama from within myself and, at the same time, sitting outside of myself.

The little man told me he knew me very well, my deepest wishes and desires. He said I wanted to know too much and asked too many questions, and that this was very dangerous. The mystery of our lives, or what we call life, should not be thought about too analytically, especially by one with so little experience. To overthink life is not the point, but I had to realize this myself. I knew he was referring to the unhealthy way, with the aid of drugs, that I was avoiding life by probing into reality with a definite bias toward self-destruction, fear, and loss.

As I watched, enthralled, I mindlessly reached forward with both hands and picked him up. He squirmed in a most repulsive way. His little arms and legs kicked and moved rapidly. I still remember the sensation of holding him. It was horrifying, touching some deep primal instinctual part of me. I recoiled in disgust and fear, dropping him to the floor. Like a piece of lead, he landed solidly on his two sturdy little feet.

My experience with this little man creature was vivid. My senses were extremely heightened and involved. I felt I was awake in a dream, where everything was so accentuated it was no longer real, so much so that reality really began to fade. I don't remember how he left or what happened after that, but I was shaken. I wasn't even high when it happened, and it was the pivotal point for me. I had lost grasp of what was real and not real, and I was frightened for my sanity.

Shortly after this incident, my mother came home for Easter and stayed about a week or so. I melted at the sight of her. My relationship with my mother never really grew up. With her, I was always a child. I felt fortunate that I was able to trust her to such a degree. Her shock and pain at the sight of my condition made me feel again. I needed her so, and she knew it and acknowledged it. Holding me, she cried, saying softly, "You need me, you need me."

I was delighted to find that I would have her all to myself because spring break from school for Steffi, Tisa, and Johnny did not coincide with her return. She lavishly doled attention on me, much to Constance's disgust. While she was home, Constance stayed at her boyfriend's apartment in the Bronx, only coming to work during the daytime. I spent hours with my mother in her bedroom, helping her organize papers, bills, and mail. I came in when she woke in the mornings, and we had breakfast together. My mother had her breakfast-in-bed ritual, and I sat by her side with my breakfast. This was more than Constance could bear, but I loved it. For once, I was not under Constance's tyranny, and I rubbed it in as best I could without my mother noticing.

My mother and I talked, and then organized my room and clothes. We got dressed and went shopping or out to lunch, or maybe ordered food in. I was an innocent child again, sharing my deepest fears and darkest thoughts, all my evils. She listened. I felt she understood exactly what I was saying and where I was coming from. But that didn't really matter. Most important, she was my mother and I could bare my soul to her. I basked in that childlike state while she was there. Her message was that I must learn from my mistakes and move on.

By the time my mother had to leave, I felt pretty good about myself. Her belief in me, the deepest me, instilled a quiet strength that helped me pull through the next few months. My mother promised she would never abandon me again, and she never did. I felt goodness again; I felt life inside of me. Nonetheless, I didn't have the know-how or a method by which I could bring myself out of this state I had gotten into. I decided to hire a tutor so I could get on track for school, using money my godfather had sent over the years. But once I started with tutoring, it felt like a cop-out. *I should be doing this myself*, I thought. I stopped going, and once again felt the letdown from high expectations. I had failed yet again. I rapidly reverted to my unhealthful patterns and bad habits.

By the beginning of summer 1965, I bought my first hit of acid. I hadn't had it before and was extremely apprehensive about taking it. I was actually terrified, but everyone I knew was using LSD.

It was my natural next step, given the course I was on. Every conversation inevitably turned to the discussion of someone's latest trip. I felt pressured to try it, as if it were my duty to expand my mind and evolve—if not for my sake, at least for humanity's.

Still, many tales of horror produced from bad trips were circulating among us, and it was unsettling. I already suffered negative effects just from pot, which was immensely milder than acid. I regularly got high with a small group of my latest buddies from the last school I had dropped out of, and we all agreed to drop the acid together. Individual acid doses in those days were very strong. We decided to take it at my family apartment, free of parents, and everyone apprehensively ate the little acid-laced sugar cubes.

We went up on the roof while we waited for it to take effect, but I vaguely felt its beginnings. We decided to go see the new Lincoln Center fountain. Word on the street was that it was amazing to see when on an acid trip. I was not so sure I liked what I was feeling, but it was very mild so far. Everyone else was excited, and colors did seem a little more intensely vivid. The thing about an acid trip is that, once you enter into it, there is no turning back. And its high can last up to fourteen hours before wearing off.

Off we all went to the main plaza of Lincoln Center. I don't remember how we got there, whether we walked or took a cab. We all gathered at the foot of the stairs leading up to the fountain in the distance. A large crowd encircled it. Lincoln Center for the Performing Arts was part of an urban renewal project, so it was new, modern, and futuristic-looking. Open sky was visible all around, a rare sight in New York. As we approached the fountain, I felt as though alien beings in an unseen spaceship hovered above us, taking people's souls and intelligence. The crowd around the fountain was about to be taken and, as in *Invasion of the Body Snatchers*, their bodies would remain inhabited by this alien intelligence. I panicked, horrified. I screamed to the others not to go near the fountain, but they didn't notice.

It appeared as if my friend George was seeing what I was seeing—he got it! Racing toward the street, he took off for a cab as fast as he could. I went with him but hesitated. We couldn't leave our friends without clearly warning them. Hysterical and in total panic, I raced toward the crowd, shouting and yelling at everyone to stay away from the fountain. I looked for our friends, but I didn't want to go deep into the crowd or close to the fountain. I raced back, and George was gone. I was alone, and the high was coming on strong. I knew I stood out along Broadway and that I must be careful not to step in front of cars. But I forgot and walked straight into oncoming traffic. Coming to, I was horrified to discover I was walking into the middle of the street. I could have stepped in front of a speeding car and been killed.

Panicked and crazy with fear, I felt I was in an alien world. Everyone looked gray. Their ears were slightly pointed, and they looked like devils. All wore trench coats or similar attire, and all were evil. It was a dark world I was in. I was aware of this, but still forgetting where I was and walking into traffic. I realized that soon I would lose complete touch with my physical reality and would not be able to get home. I managed to flag down a man in a red sports car. Screaming, I begged him to please take me to my address on Central Park West before it was too late. My moments in lucidity were running out. Fortunately the driver of the sports car took me right to my door and made sure I got upstairs.

I went into the apartment, and George and the others were there. George was crying and staying close to his friend Paul, whom he trusted. I envied him; I trusted no one. I knew that not even my mother would be of help to me at this point. I felt completely alone as the high continued to take over, and we had many hours to go. The fear I felt is indescribable. I entered a world with no time and where a moment is eternal. I felt my body melting into everything, but not into the ecstatic oneness of divinity but in a drastic toxic sort of way, like the Wicked Witch melting in *The Wizard of Oz*. The high was the opposite of nature and beauty, and my body was melting and becoming one with a toxic world. A physical and structural transformation was taking place, necessary for me to enter this underworld fully. Otherwise my body would have been incapable of sustaining the unimaginable and infinite horror it was about to experience.

I was becoming one with evil, the devil, but not as fear, which is merely an attribute of it, but as evil itself. By choosing to take LSD, I had chosen to become one with the acid and give myself to it. It was a done deal. There was no way out and no turning back. It was too late, *way* too late. I felt a terror at the realization of this finality. Once I reached this point of no return, it felt as if my body was gone and I was left in hell for all eternity. I was there to fully experience horrors upon horrors, beyond comprehension, not limited by the body, which loses consciousness at a certain unendurable point. There is no limit to the pain one can feel in hell. This is the place I was. It was no good to scream or yell. I was in hell, with the devil himself.

The mythological monster Medusa was spread out, with snakes coming from her head and entwining her whole body, surrounded by nymphs and little creatures and intricate patterns of vines. She was sketched on the top of a very large coffee table in the living room of our apartment. Its legs were thick, square, and black. Under its glass top was a green color of watery texture, like the scales of a fish reflecting light but at the same time having depth. There was endless detail. I mention this table because it is very symbolic of what was happening to me. I sat for at least eight hours, during the height of my high, staring at this table. My mind, or maybe it was my intellect, continued to chatter. It wove one empty word and concept after another. It was the devil, personified, speaking to me as I understood him.

Lost in a senseless maze of the mind with an endless variety of argument or nonsense available to it, I realized I was in insanity. Terror gripped me. I saw no way out. How could I ever find my way back when I did not know what was real or not real? My hold on reality was already shaky without the LSD. I had no sense of trust. I was totally isolated. Everything and everybody was a part of my own mind. I was dwelling in a state of absolute self-centeredness. Anything that happened, any noise, any walking in the room, all was part of my insanity. It all had meaning for only me in my complete despotism, self-indulgence as far as it could go. I experienced the notion of certainty that I would never reach reality again. It was lost to me forever.

Late into the next day and early evening, as the high wore off and I was no longer bound completely to my tripped-out mind, I walked about as though I were the devil incarnate. My hands, my skin, my face—all were him. There was nothing I could do about it; I had been initiated. I had entered hell, met the devil, and become one with him. I learned the intimacies of his mind and spent hours listening to him. I had met insanity, for if there is no love, it is *all* insane. I felt, in my being, the incarnation of innocence's opposite. As the evening went into night and night wore on into early morning, I still could not sleep or escape. I roamed as an animal, a devil, throughout the apartment.

The high wore off, but gradually, as if coming out of a metamorphosis and regaining my identity, like a werewolf becoming human again. As my consciousness heightened, I was very aware of the slow process of change.

At the first dawning of light, someone in the next room put on a record of "Ave Maria." In the room I was in, the windows were very high and large, and the sun was coming up to the background music. It was a sign of hope for me. By the end of the angelic hymn, I was finally able to feel again.

I cried and cried, so grateful. Even so, a terrible emptiness remained inside of me. What had I done? Was it irreversible? Did my soul get sold to the devil? Because the music was so beatific, and the light outside so large and real—even though my mind argued that I belonged to the devil—I was able at that moment to bypass the negative self-talk and its devious logic and really sense true hope.

sixteen

Phase Transition

After the bad acid trip, I vowed to never take drugs again. I decided to change the direction of my life, as I was truly shaken, and dedicate my life to God. I had to be forgiven by God, even if it took my whole lifetime. I had to feel assurance that what I had done was not irreparable. God and redemption were on my mind constantly.

Anyone who has experienced a bad acid trip knows it can take years to overcome the effects of that trauma and its accompanying flashbacks. Perceptions I had of hell, the devil's presence within me, visual flashes, and many other horrors related to that trip resurfaced many times throughout my days. I heard the sounds of hell and felt an ominous presence, and once again I forgot my attachment with the world. I was constantly terrified. I knew my concept of reality was unstable and fragile. I was certain that if I did another trip, I would go insane indefinitely. People constantly dropped acid, and I lived in terror that someone might, to be generous or as a joke, slip me some. That would be my doom.

During the acid trip, I experienced such fear that afterward I had the sensation of blown fuses in my heart and emotional center as if all the wires were frayed. In the months that followed, the slightest hint of fear took over my entire body, like an electric current. I was so scared by what I felt, worsening matters. My heart area burned wildly, and my whole sense of reality lost its grounding. I'd allowed my world to be invaded and entirely taken over by fear. What I had experienced was so far-out that I was sure only God could help repair me.

I trusted no one anymore, not even my mother. As I said earlier, I left my mother at the threshold of that first LSD trip. Like many teens, I didn't feel comfortable reaching out to my elders, who couldn't possibly understand. Even I didn't comprehend the impact of our trips and their toll on us, so how could an adult comprehend the extent of the detriment of it? I felt no respect, no awe, and no interest in the ambitions associated with our society. I saw no reason to live for those objectives. So what if a person is successful? What does it mean anyway? Life was void to me, meaningless. I couldn't conceive of living in what I saw as futility. No one seemed to question why he or she was doing anything, just going mindlessly through the moves, and yet a whole monstrous social structure was built on what seemed like thin air.

I knew I had to live. I wanted to live, *needed* to live. But for what? Society's designs meant nothing to me. I had lived a very indulgent and selfish life. I wanted freedom from that, whatever it took. I needed peace, and I needed life to be meaningful. I wanted to feel passion and be part of a picture bigger than my own selfish interests, the vision I saw that morning as the sun's light splashed so brightly across the sky.

I wanted the life that fills babies with awe. I wanted to be a part of that world in which we're all one, God's world. I had to find God. I had to be forgiven. I had to be a part of Him, a part of something much bigger than my own selfish interests. There was really nothing for me out in the average world, nothing. And the constant recurrence of my nightmare trip made me desperate to discover life again.

On a soul level, I was dead. I felt nothing. When I saw love around me, such as people holding hands or kittens playing, I could not relate. It didn't make sense to me intellectually. Without the ability to really feel, I had difficulty understanding why or what was happening. I had forgotten how to process emotion. It was like love had been deleted from my database, as if I were missing a sensitivity chip. All I knew was that I needed God to put life back into me.

For the next year, I suspiciously observed my surroundings, not trusting nor relating to anyone. I saw adults as adolescent and frivolous, trying to regain their youth. I saw my peers as shallow, insensitive—they accepted way too many things as given without questioning them. I didn't like their world, and I didn't belong in it. Still, in some way, I envied them all. I was the one who had lost innocence. I could no longer just live to live, do things to do things. By inquisitively examining everything, I had cut my umbilical cord with life. It's true, in this way, that ignorance is bliss.

But what *did* I want? I only knew God would make everything all right, and I tried to live my life in continuous prayer. I abstained from anything I felt was wrong, whether object or action. I behaved well and returned to school in the fall of 1965, at seventeen years old. I did homework perhaps for the first time ever.

But the impetus behind all this change was fear, not love of God. I was scared out of my wits. Everything scared me, all the time. I saw a bag lady mumbling to herself on the street and thought, *That could be my future.* All things negative seemed so close, so real. It was a lot easier to just keep on sliding like before. Facing life seemed an unimaginably insurmountable feat. I would never make it—I didn't have the strength.

My only source of energy was my tremendous fear. Ironically, the fear is what ultimately drove me out of the sludge. It was a long slow process and extremely painful. Just getting out of bed and doing dishes were unbelievably difficult feats. All my ambitions were set on just getting little chores of life done. I prayed as I stood over the sink washing dishes. It took everything I had. I thought in wonderment what it might be like if doing chores was just second nature to me. I had deep admiration for everyone around me— they were able to live functionally. How strong they must be. I set my sights on seemingly simple goals that, to me, felt like scaling a tall building or scoring a million dollars.

It was several years before I was comfortable taking care of basic household chores. My second big challenge was to just be like anyone else, normal, not a misfit. I had to someday finish school. But back in the fall of 1965, I was just getting by, shuffling two steps forward and falling one step back, depleting all my strength. But a fire was lit under me by all that fear, and I had to move ahead, excruciating as it was.

I completely lacked comprehension skills in school and had very little idea what was going on. I had no study habits. One of my first weeks in school, I had an assignment to write an essay as part of a test. It was required to be three hundred words in length, but I found I could answer the essay question in about ten words. I tried paraphrasing my writing in different ways, thinking it was the only possible way I could hope to fill the page. The teacher took one look at my paper and made me an appointment with the school psychologist. I wanted to run, but I couldn't do that anymore. I had to face the humiliation, most of which was self-inflicted.

I dragged myself to school every day. I never believed I would make it again the next day, but I did, to my own astonishment. At my new school, I met some kindred souls. I attended Professional Children's School, in our Upper West Side neighborhood. It's a performing and visual arts school, so enrollment required that students work professionally in the arts. In my case, my experience with modeling fulfilled the school's requirement.

My mother encouraged me to model to earn some income and feel better about myself. I hated it. I never liked being photographed. Modeling could not have been a worse fit for me. My older sister Mia, at twenty-one, was gaining enormous attention in the press over her relationship with Frank Sinatra. This did not help either. By the time Mia had reached eighteen several years earlier, she was already an accomplished actress starring in the hit television soap *Peyton Place*. She was ambitious, beautiful, and smart, and knew where she was going. The opposite of me, I felt. Nonetheless, my time at the school was lifesaving.

I met a classmate my age named Lily, a successful model. She ran away from her Ohio home when she was sixteen. She now lived with her boyfriend in the East Village. I visited her apartment often, and we became close friends. She had been through as much as I had, in her own way, and was modeling to support herself. I also met Charles, also our age, going on eighteen, a professional musician attending Juilliard School of Music. He was the most sensitive person I had ever met, and we had fascinating conversations.

Later in the school year, a new boy, Eric, came to my school. His mother was a psychologist who had raised him for a time in Mexico, where she worked closely with Timothy Leary. Timothy Leary was perhaps the most influential counterculture figure of the '60s. He advocated the use of psychedelic drugs for expanding consciousness. He is famous for saying, "turn on, tune in, drop out." Eric was a couple years younger, but fascinating. He took his first acid trip at age eight, under the supervision of his mother and Leary. His perception was noticeably different from others'. Conversations with him went on for hours, and everything he said was from a novel perspective. I couldn't get enough of him, soaking up his unique insights.

My friends were inspirational and supportive, and I grew stronger because of them. I actually developed some study skills in school, and I became increasingly excited. By January of 1966, when turning 18, I no longer felt all of life was insurmountable. Each day was a little bit better than the day before it.

One afternoon while in my bedroom, forcing myself to study, an ethereal wisp of joy streamed past my mind's eye. I immediately noticed it, a thin column, like smoke drifting up from the lit end of a cigarette. I jumped on it like a cat after a mouse, but it evaporated. It was subtle, but in contrast to the months I felt dried up, empty, and dead inside, it might as well have been a flashing neon sign.

That this joy came from inside was not lost on me. I was already deeply moved by Eastern thought, which claims the strength and vision of our entire outer world is a direct reflection of the strength and vision of our inner consciousness. I had read about meditation in *Siddhartha*, the book Tom had gifted to me. This latest experience rekindled my interest in it.

I scoured the many obscure little occult bookstores scattered throughout '60s-era New York. I read everything I could find on every possible form of meditation—Zen, yogic, Sufi, Rosicrucian. I even tried using a mirrored disc I mail-ordered. I was to stare into it to direct my attention deeply inward. Then Eric told me his mother studied Zen meditation, and I went with him to a little apartment on the far Upper East Side where a small gathering of budding Buddhists sat to meditate together. With no instruction, I was unable to gauge what I was doing. We all just meditated, whatever that meant exactly. Dissatisfied, I continued passionately searching. I was sure something more was out there.

By spring, I was noticeably different. Although anxiety and fear were still with me, they were less potent. I still suffered from bouts of depression, but its hold on me was diminishing. I realized that my actions, behaviors, thoughts, and emotions were all in constant dialogue with God. He was speaking to me and supporting me through my successes, failures, relationships, achievements, and even mundane activities. I felt wisps of hope grow stronger. I had to keep trying, no matter how painful or seemingly futile. This was the way I would grow to Him.

By spring of 1966, my life was more positive. I still was way behind in school, but if I attended summer school and passed some extra-credit tests, there was a good chance I would be caught up enough to graduate. I couldn't believe it. I was by no means at college-prep level, but I would graduate high school. My mother was so proud. My newly acquired study methods, tricks, and tools had worked. I now understood the learning process. I could write a paper, read stories, and memorize formulas. As summer came around and school ended, I felt even more hopeful.

My constant prayer was to be shown a way to commit my life to God. I didn't know how it would happen, but I believed it would work out. Early in the summer, I was invited on a car trip out of the city with a friend. He was several years older and studying physics at Harvard. I had been in the city for so long, it seemed as though the whole world was covered in cement.

To my great surprise and delight, I saw vast stretches of green rolling hills and trees. The richness of scent, sight, and sound was uplifting. It was so beautiful. The soft sweet country air, even if filled with insects, was so enticing. I had almost forgotten nature's beauty. Every pore of my being drank it in. The house we visited was cedar wood built multilayered with several floors among the treetops, where fewer insects resided and breezes blew freely. From one of its two large open porches, I gazed at the vast sky and its endless horizon, a sea of all shades of green. We sat outside on the larger of the wooden porches, which wrapped delicately around the topmost floor of the house, carefully avoiding the trunks of the taller trees. It was a lovely welcoming evening.

As I sat contentedly, watching the sun fade below the trees, I had a subtle feeling of recognition. Someone came around the corner from behind me, reaching out to hand me a pill. I had decided a year earlier that I would never touch another drug. I was so strong in my conviction that I told a friend I would rather be hung by my fingernails and have my skin slowly peeled off than take another trip. I would not have taken it, but this particular evening, the person giving the pill was heralded by a profound spiritual presence that overtook my being. I'm sure the person with the pill was not aware of this. I knew I had no choice but to obey. It is hard to describe. I asked the young woman what I had taken. She said, "You are taking mescaline, the hallucinogenic property of peyote."

I sat in blind submission as this hallowed presence invaded every part of my being, but it was gentle. I was safe. I felt the same familiar spiritual sensation seeping into my soul that I experienced when my father died. I sat alone, staring out into the darkening quiet. The silence of the forest and mountains poured over me, seeping through the wooden floorboards and filling the porch. The prior background music of crickets, frogs, owls, and wind-through-the-trees receded completely. I felt peace and satisfaction gently well up inside me. It was like I was participating in my own graduation of sorts, my rite of passage. I had survived my walk-about successfully and earned the right to be here.

Something momentous was to take place, a confirmation per-haps, propelling me into the next phase, a new beginning. I can't really explain why I was so certain of this. As I sat watching the shadowed tops of the trees, I felt a sense of destiny. I was startled abruptly by a sudden loud rumbling and shaking, like a subway car approaching its station, only with no sound. I sat up with a sud-den realization: *It's time—it's coming!* Before I could consciously ask myself what was coming, all the hair on my body felt as if it were standing on end, only it wasn't hair—it was my body's energies.

A voice in my mind shouted, "Look over there!" I looked ahead into the darkness and realized my eyes were closed. In the dis-tance, a comet, very small but rapidly expanding, headed toward me. I didn't see it—I *felt* it, a mass of energy hurtling toward me. I froze.

It came at lightning speed, engulfing me entirely like a blan-ket. It felt as if a huge strobe light went off in my brain and filled it with holy sacred silence. I was suddenly separated from my mind and its infinite nonstop flow of chatter, imaginations, and illusions, like a rocket disconnects from its burned-out engines and moves silently away into timeless frictionless space. Passing out of my in-tellect and beyond, transitioning away, I watched as the chatter of my mind receded as it grew smaller and less significant. It was like being in the heart of the city amid confusion, chaos, horns honk-ing, brakes screeching, people talking and shouting, then slowly being lifted up past it toward the sky, passing by the giant skyscrap-ers that seemed so large from below and now were miniature. I watched something that was not me fade into the distance.

My intellect, which had entrapped me for so long, scared me, and entangled me in its web of so-called reality, was now harmless—it wasn't me and never was. It was small and petty. I remembered who I really was, who I am and have always been. As I continued to move away from the smallness of my mind, the dimensions of my spirit exponentially multiplied, encompassing each and every living creature past, present, and future. They were infinitely many and yet one. It was incomprehensible in its vastness and proportions, but I knew it intimately.

In a flash, I touched God. At that instant, a bolt of lightning pierced through the dark blanket of sky above as if to confirm the power I tapped. Thunder crackled. I couldn't move or talk for several hours, catatonic in my friend's arms. I was aware of what was going on around me but was unable to respond in any way. I had left my body and needed time to reorient back into it.

Gradually, as I reentered physical consciousness, I was aware there had been a message—I would find what I was looking for in two months and know it when I saw it, and I would meet an Indian master, my master. I also remembered hearing music, South Asian chanting. The next day, when I described it to my new friends at the tree house, they told me what I was describing sounded like Indian or Tibetan chants.

I returned to New York in high spirits, piquing the interest of my siblings. Had I fallen in love? Whom had I met? I tried to convey to my youngest sister the amazing experience and how in two months I would find what I was looking for and know it when I saw it. She didn't get it, and somehow, trying to explain it to her and put it into words cheapened it. I decided not to tell anyone else and quietly held it close to me, deep inside. My buddy, George, my friend from my LSD trip, kept asking what I had taken because he saw a difference in me and wanted it too.

seventeen

Hope Emerges

I managed to finish that year of high school, but I did not graduate for I still lacked some necessary credits. My mother arranged for me to leave New York and work with the Kenley Players, a prestigious summer stock theater group in Ohio. John Kenley ran a large operation of very successful stage shows in Dayton, Columbus, Toledo, Cleveland, and Warren. I went to Columbus and enjoyed my time there, although short-lived. Most of my fellow players had never known anyone like me, an anomaly. I practiced meditation, slept on the floor, ate vegetarian food, read Buddhist scriptures, followed the *I Ching*, burned incense, and prayed a lot.

My mother wanted all her children to be in show business, like the Barrymore family, she said. Mia was the only one who really wanted to be an actress. My mother saw this summer job as an opportunity for me to get a leg up—or "break a leg" as they say in the biz—by gaining acting experience in a few professional shows. My roommate in Ohio was Heather MacRae, daughter of well-known stage star Gordon MacRae. Heather later starred in several Broadway shows, and her older sister was a well-known TV actress. I knew I was very fortunate to have this opportunity, but I had no interest in acting. I chose to work in the props department instead. We did grand shows, like the musical *Kismet*, starring Heather's father, with a full live orchestra. Other stars, such as Richard Chamberlain, performed while I was there.

When John Kenley came through to visit the Columbus theater, he asked why I chose to work in props. I told him I did not want to act. He encouraged me to continue on and see how I felt after a month or two. When my feelings had not changed after six weeks, he explained that hundreds of young people wanted the position I was filling. I told him to give it to one of them, since my feelings about acting were not going to change. John Kenley was a very talented and interesting man, who happened also to be a hermaphrodite. In winter, when summer stock was off-season, she lived in Florida and her name was Joan.

I parted in good stead and went to California to stay with my brother Patrick. There was something magical about the way he approached life. He had just come back from living in Baja with his new wife, who was pregnant with their first child. He believed simpler was better, living in an abandoned restaurant in Malibu, along the Pacific Coast Highway, on a cliff overlooking the sea. The building ran north and south, parallel to the water. He and his wife had the southern section, and another couple lived in the northern side. My brother met his wife, Susan, in Vermont, both artists who made their home beautiful with many colorful drawings, paintings, and handwoven wall hangings.

Susan had a loom and wove her own cloth. I loved being in their home. The couple next door was very colorful. The young woman had just done a cover spread for *Playboy* magazine and was chosen Playmate of the Year. Her boyfriend had long hair past his waist and walked around naked. I never saw him wear clothes.

One afternoon while perched on a massive rock on the cliff overlooking the sea, I read my large Rosicrucian book. The Rosicrucian Order was a mystical philosophy founded in the early 1400s in Germany by a physician and philosopher who spent many years in the Middle East. It is said to have its origins in ancient

Sufism. I was interested in this book because of its meditation. My brother's friend Peter walked by on his way to visit. As he neared I felt the same subtle sensation as earlier in the summer in the cedar tree house in upstate New York, a gentle presence of profound silence and connectedness. He asked what I was reading. As I looked up to respond, I knew right away something larger was happening. I answered that I was reading about meditation. He said he knew just the thing for me. He had been to India, where he met a great yogi and sage named Maharishi Mahesh Yogi who taught a yoga meditation called Transcendental Meditation, referred to as TM for short.

He described a method of diving inward, "transcending," a way of going deep inside the mind and connecting with a reservoir at its base of silent bliss. Tapping into this brings a little out each time. His explanation was sublime, so simple and direct by comparison to the many practices I had read about and tried. Other practices spoke of controlling the mind, mastering it through concentration, clearing it of thoughts through discipline and focus. These methods were hard work for some and took a lot of time, even years, to get results that were truly transformative.

Peter was describing something so supremely simple. When I asked how he controlled the mind enough to make it go inward, he replied that there was no control. "How can that be?" I asked. "The mind certainly does not go inward naturally. I have tried and tried."

He replied, "Exactly, you have tried too hard. It's like diving when swimming. It doesn't work until you get the correct angle, no matter how hard you try. But once you get that angle, your body slips through into the water as gravity takes over. In TM, the teacher gives you the correct angle through technique and a mental tool, and the mind itself slips inward through its own gravity, which is the natural tendency of the mind to go toward more."

"So, you're saying the mind itself does the transcending. There is no effort?"

"Correct. It goes inward because it wants to. We just have to show it how. Another way to think of it is the technique and the mental tool that the student is given by the teacher are kind of like a shoehorn, where you just set the heel up correctly and it slips in on its own."

This was brilliant to me. Every step of the way was so intelligently explained. And after taking the meditation course, I found no stone left unturned. Every experience was explained—how it happens in the meditation process and how it is integrated into our lives outside of meditation. There was no question that could not be answered and understood. I was amazed. No other technique of meditation I knew had provided this thorough an understanding of itself and its method.

Besides the simplicity of this technique, what sets it apart from other meditative processes is the transcending it offers, its method of diving within and directly accessing deep inner silence.

This is what I was looking for—and it was exactly two months since my prophetic experience in the summer. I could not believe I was finally finding the method of meditation I dreamed of. What I didn't know was that this was merely the beginning.

I asked Peter how he wound up in India in the first place. He told me that he and my brother, when they were younger, went to the Mojave Desert, outside of Los Angeles, to eat magic mushrooms together. A few months after they returned from the desert, Peter said he went into a similar state as in the desert, only he had not eaten any mushrooms or taken drugs. He described this state as a cosmic state, a very blissful experience that lasted about two weeks. He said that, during this time, he kept serendipitously hearing about a great woman saint in India named Sri Anandamayi Ma.

Then someone he randomly met told him the blessings he was experiencing during these two weeks were from the Divine Mother, and he would find her in the form of a woman saint in India named Sri Anandamayi Ma. Stunned, Peter pursued and pressed this person as to why he would tell him this. The person had no recollection of saying it. Peter took his college money, much to the dismay of his parents, and traveled to India in 1963 to meet this woman saint.

Peter spent six amazing months around her, mostly in northern India in Hardwar, her main residence. She told him he needed to study in Rishikesh with a great saint, Maharishi Mahesh Yogi, who knew about Westerners. Reluctantly, Peter left her, feeling forlorn, confused, and abandoned. He took the forty-five minute bus ride up to Rishikesh, nestled in the foothills of the Himalayas. Rishikesh is a known sacred pilgrimage spot especially suited for meditation. About a mile outside of Rishikesh, he felt the same exquisite silence he had experienced emanating from Anandamayi Ma. There was no difference. When he met Maharishi, he humbly surrendered himself.

Peter told me intriguing stories of his time in India, how he spent timeless hours in meditation under Maharishi's guidance. He saw Maharishi meet with many visiting sages and ascetics. Maharishi placed his hands over the heart of one of them, and huge strobe flashes of light emanated outward. Unimaginable bliss and peace emanated from these great timeless sages. I was mesmerized by any tidbit he could tell me, no matter how small.

Before I learned TM, Peter took me to a home not far from the beach, where I met people and observed them meditating. We entered a stucco building, and Peter led me into the back of a room cleared of furniture. A small group of about nine or ten older people sat quietly in rows. We came in a little late, just as they were beginning. I looked around the room and saw people my mother's age—no one appeared to be even *near* our age. I tried not to form judgments, but I felt out of place. I sat watching, not knowing what to think as Peter and the others sat incredibly still for a half hour. My mind raced when I suddenly noticed an eerie feeling, which lasted for about twenty minutes, as if they had all left and I was alone in the room. I kept trying to recapture that amazing spiritual presence from my past experiences, but I felt nothing. Perhaps I was trying too hard to make it happen instead of allowing it.

After meditation, the group listened to a nearly inaudible tape recording of the Indian yogi speaking and laughing. I could barely hear or decipher his accent, wondering how they could sit so rapt. All the while, I was distracted by the fact that all the people there were unduly average and middle-aged. They were dressed conservatively, the men in suits and ties, the women with short dyed bouffant hairdos. This was hardly what I expected or wanted. After the meeting, I pounced on Peter with questions about these people. Who were they? Why were they there? To me, they represented a culture of people who didn't understand me, one I wanted to leave behind.

Peter, unperturbed and laughing, answered that I was being superficial. These people were different, he told me. "Then why do they choose to dress and wear their hair in ways that support what we don't believe in?" I asked. He said it was more complicated, that if they fit in they could do more good than if they stand out, kind of like spies. Peter always seemed to have an answer, and I was grateful. He also pointed out that I can't judge people by appearance.

That evening Peter introduced me to Jerry Jarvis, the man who became my Transcendental Meditation teacher. Although he was conservatively dressed and with short hair, Jerry was not in a stuffy jacket-and-tie getup and, at thirty-two, was clearly younger than the others. He wore a white T-shirt showing under the open collar of his work shirt. He was a landscape gardener and reminded me of my oldest brother Michael, who had passed on. Jerry was very friendly, with a great smile. I liked him, and there was something very different about him.

I didn't know what it would entail, having Jerry as my teacher. I was in a kind of daze. It was all a tad overwhelming for me. I couldn't believe this was finally happening. I had dreamed of it too long. The momentum building over the next two weeks brought everything to a high pitch. Peter came around a lot and answered my barrage of questions: Why a formal course if it's so simple? Where did this technique come from? Who was Jerry's Indian teacher? How did the saint, Maharishi Mahesh Yogi, learn? What did meditation have to do with yoga? What's the difference between Zen and yogic meditation? On and on.

By the time the course started, I was lightheaded from excitement. The course lasted six weeks, meeting every Tuesday and Thursday evening. Peter, almost as excited as I was, came with me to all the meetings. All his meditating friends popped into various evening sessions, and I liked them all. About thirty people were in the course, which was held in a large science classroom at UCLA. The entrance to class was at the top of the room, slanting steeply downward to a lecture podium. I sat in the top row. The lectures were amazing. Every step and stage was unique, excellently explained by Jerry. There were moments I wanted to weep in gratitude and appreciation.

The day of my initiation into TM finally came on a beautiful Saturday morning in mid-August at a rented office for the budding student TM organization on Gayley Street in Westwood. I was one of the first to be instructed that day. We were asked to bring flowers, fruit, and a handkerchief. Peter had taken me to his parents' garden to choose several of his mother's best flowers, one of which was bird-of-paradise.

As I entered the room, not knowing quite what to expect, I was welcomed by Jerry's beaming face. Sitting to meditate, I closed my eyes. I felt as if the instruction itself had little to do with the teacher. It was almost as if he weren't there and I was waking something innately in me. Immediately, slipping seamlessly past thought, I watched as my attention glided through various layers of consciousness, finally disappearing deep into transcendental silence. This happened many times. It was not flashy, as I had expected.

As I explained my experience to Jerry, I could not help showing some confusion. I loved the peace and quiet bliss, but I expected a more revelatory experience instead of a quiet and unassuming process. Still, I knew the profundity of what I was experiencing. He said emphatically, "Exactly, this is what you want. Now let's see what the effects of it are on you."

I responded proudly, "I think finding this deep resource inside is ultimately the answer for all of humanity."

Jerry continued, "Yes, but finding it is not all there is to it. There is something more important than finding it."

"No, there is not. I can assure you," I said, authoritatively.

He answered, "There is something better. It is living it, and that is what you are learning to do."

I noticed a change that very day. Although subtle, a priority shift had quietly taken place. Time took on new meaning, suddenly becoming far more precious to me—I couldn't waste it anymore. I felt compelled to use it much more wisely. I realized this had to be a result of my meditation. I also noticed my thoughts, inordinately dominant since my marijuana days, were significantly more subdued. What remained of my LSD flashback receded further, and I became more aware of the need to heal deeply. I still suffered from bouts of intense stress, fear, and lack of confidence in my ability to embrace a future and my true self.

My sister Mia was enormously famous after marrying Frank Sinatra in 1966 at age twenty-one. She quickly rose in celebrity as a leading actress, starring in films of the 1960s and '70s, such as *Secret Ceremony, Rosemary's Baby, John and Mary, Follow Me!, The Great Gatsby*, and *Death on the Nile*. A dozen Woody Allen films followed through the 1980s and '90s.

I often felt Mia's fame usurped my identity, in a sense, my life overshadowed, stolen. I didn't want her experience, but everyone saw me in terms of it. People openly wondered aloud, "What happened to you? Why aren't you successful like her?" Still, through it all, I knew I was my worst enemy and that if I could get strong, the rest would take care of itself. This is where TM came in.

I needed to live and get beyond all this. I craved the healing silence I tapped into daily. All I thought of was, *How can I go study in India with this master sage and yogi, Maharishi, founder of this amazing technique of meditation?* TM was a revolutionary tool, with the potential to change the world, transforming humanity one person at a time. I still feel this way, perhaps even more so since I've now been practicing and teaching the method for years. I was obsessive with meditation before I discovered TM, but now I was taking it to a new level. I eagerly wanted to learn more. I knew it was the solution to all my problems and that it was all I wanted.

At the end of summer, my mother arranged for me to go to finishing school in Florence, Italy. I knew no one who followed this archaic method of training young women, but I followed her desires. I was not yet entirely on my own. I learned Maharishi was giving a course beginning January 1967, for three months in Rishikesh, India. While passing through London on my way to Florence, I applied for the course. I received word that I was too young. I needed to be twenty-four and a college graduate. This was a terrible blow. How could I possibly wait six long years? And *college?* I was deflated by the response and did not know what to do.

My school was at the home of an Italian family, run by the mother. She had one daughter, about a year younger than I was. There were six other American girls at my school. After settling in our rooms the first day, we had our orientation meeting and were told about our fall schedules. We would attend university in the mornings to learn Italian and be taken on tours in the afternoons to see all the great works of art. (I was there just before the devastating 1966 Arno River flood, which destroyed millions of masterpieces in Florence.) We would receive music lessons in the evenings, for a refined lady should play a musical instrument. One girl would learn the harp, another, the mandolin, and so on. I was informed that I would learn bass. Bass did not seem very ladylike to me. When I asked, why bass? I was told it suited me. I felt insulted even though it is an amazing musical instrument.

Although I had nothing in common with the other girls, I had good rapport with the mother. She watched me go regularly to meditate. One evening at her behest, I told her about meditation and how there was a real saint in India I longed to meet and study with. She shared her religious experiences. My need for a more profound spiritual life haunted my days and nights. I had to somehow get to India.

Being Catholic, I decided I needed a miracle. I packed my bags, leaving most of my clothes and belongings behind in Florence, and took off on my little scooter that I had bought weeks earlier for Lourdes. It had been eight years since I was there with my family at age ten. I arrived with a few clothes, a pair of shoes, and my favorite boots, which were promptly stolen upon my arrival in Lourdes. I camped out at first in what appeared to be a wild patch of land downstream from the grotto, a few miles along the rapid rushing river that runs along it. I found that every place I set up camp, no matter how wild and uninhabited it appeared, some un-foreseen person or family always owned it. So I found a small room for rent in a boarding house. My parents had left a trust fund for my education, so I fortunately did not feel the pressure of money issues.

Once settled in Lourdes, what I thought would be a one-week stay turned into two and a half months. I arrived in late September after the tourist season ended, the perfect time to be there, when the town becomes inhabited by religious orders. My first day in the boarding house, I found to my delight that the owners treated guests like family. They provided all meals during my stay, even packing lunches for me to take to the grotto. The owners' daughter, who was about twenty-four, spoke perfect English. She and I became friends, and I appreciated her warmth.

I immediately got into a routine of going daily to early morning mass at 6:00 a.m. in the Basilica of the Rosary just above the grotto, then going to the grotto to meditate and pray until lunch. After lunch, I bathed in the waters and then meditated and prayed again in the grotto. I loved hearing the sound of Latin echoing through the halls of the great basilica in the early mornings, as the numerous chapels lining its walls filled with priests and monks performing and reciting individual mass. I was particularly fascinated by the recluse orders of nuns, who covered their faces with veils and prayed on their knees all day long in the little hidden chapels. I loved my stay there.

Before I left Los Angeles, Peter loaned me beads that Indian saint Sri Anandamayi Ma had worn, flowers she had blessed, and a book of her quotes. She'd held the book on her lap over several days for Peter. I slept every night with the flowers and book under my pillow. In Lourdes, every day before and after meditation, I read from the book. Sometimes I opened it randomly to see what the message was. Every time I did that, it was appropriate. I also prayed the rosary many times during the day.

My first afternoon in Lourdes, I went down to the rushing Gave de Pau, the river just below the grotto, to eat my lunch, a fresh baguette with a slab of cheese, and an apple. I found a perfect spot, just off to the side. An Irish priest, also planning to eat his lunch by the river, approached me. Apparently, I was in his usual spot. He had been in Lourdes for three weeks, and we struck up a conversation. I told him about my meditation and how it was a yogic practice from India. He launched into a sermon about the dangers of spiritual practices from traditions we do not understand. He added that yoga was considered a practice of devil worship.

I ignored his predictable response and changed the subject. We had good conversation, laughing and having fun. But secretly, he was not going to let my soul be lost to devil worship. He continued his crusade to save me. At first I thought his attention harmless. Then I found it annoying—he did not let up. When he brought in others who also made it their cause, I got angry and avoided them. But sometime after their continued assaults, in a weakened state I entertained the possibility that everything I believed was really a trick of the devil.

As I sat one day in the grotto to meditate, I thought it would be just like me to sit in one of the most sacred and holy places on earth and inadvertently worship the devil. I was gripped by fear, once again. Profoundly conflicted, I needed direction to know what was right. I prayed all the harder, explaining in my prayers that I didn't need a big miracle but just a sign.

Finally, I decided I would go to confession. Perhaps the priest would provide some peace in this matter. I attended confession and bared my soul. This was a big mistake. I was told I must immediately stop my practice of meditation. Hanging on by a thread to my beloved meditation practice, I went before Our Lady, who represents the Divine Mother of us all. I pleaded with her to guide me. With great trepidation, mustering all my courage, I decided to meditate one last time in the grotto.

Many times, I sat to meditate and pray in the grotto over the last months but was nudged out by minor provocations. Any number of groups took over the grotto for private prayer sessions, masses, or weddings. This particular morning, I vaguely heard a shuffle of feet emptying and filling the wooden pews around me. I continued to meditate. Suddenly, loud male voices beside me were singing the mass in Latin. I opened my eyes to see cardinals, archbishops, and bishops all around. I looked up at the one singing next to me and was met with a beatific smile. I closed my eyes and respectfully finished my meditation, uninterrupted, and this had never happened before. The grotto had been cleared of all its other worshipers for a special high mass conducted by and for an assembly of visiting Catholic dignitaries, but remarkably I was left unnoticed in their midst. I now knew, deep in my heart, that all was well. Feeling peaceful, I left Lourdes knowing all my prayers were heard and answered.

eighteen

Sustaining Hope: Biding My Time

When I returned from Lourdes to New York, I stayed with my mother in her apartment, arriving home in the evening. Earlier that day, a representative of the Brazilian chapter of my mother's fan club had visited. When the woman heard I was coming from Europe, she drew a lovely picture of the sky and ocean all in blue. When I went into my room, I saw this large blue drawing with the words, "Welcome Home," and it was signed, "Lourdes"! The woman's name was Lourdes, and I had never before met anyone with that name. When I saw the words all bathed in blue, which is the color of the Divine Mother, I knew instantly my request to go and study with Maharishi in India was given approval. It was a done deal, even though I had no idea how it would happen.

I stayed with my mother longer than anticipated. My two younger sisters still lived at home. I didn't know what to do with myself because meditation was my great love and only interest. My mother also didn't know what to do with me. I sat to meditate twice a day for a half hour each time, and my worried mother complained I was trying to escape from life. Frustrated, she yelled that closing my eyes to life would get me nowhere fast. One morning, when I was meditating before an appointment, my mother couldn't stand it anymore. She came into the room where I was sitting and poured an entire bucket of water over my head.

She took me to see a psychiatrist. He told me that if I didn't stop this dangerous nonsense, I could lose my mind. The psychiatrist showed me pictures of naked *sadhus* and ascetics covered in ash, their hair matted in dreadlocks all the way to the ground. "Is this what you want to happen to you?" he asked me. "Do you really want to be a zombie? Because this is where you are headed, young lady."

My mother genuinely believed my daily meditating was more dangerous and destructive than LSD. Still, my devotion and desire to learn more were unyielding. My mother and the psychiatrist made me an offer. Feeling my desire for God and meditation were unhealthy and merely a means of escapism, they gave me two choices: 1) I could go to a special school in Vermont, where I would learn necessary life skills, or 2) I could go to a special hospital nearby in White Plains, New York, and take time to realize I needed proper direction.

I knew the mental hospital would be far more difficult. But I thought if I chose the more difficult path, I would receive a greater blessing or more personal growth. I chose that mental hospital, which turned out to be far more frightening than I had imagined. The hospital had graded levels. I never went to the lower levels but at night, in particular, I heard the howling of people in mental anguish.

I was put in the second highest level, filled mostly with alcoholic women and wealthy "problem" girls whose parents could not control them. Some tried to run away. They got caught and were taken to a lower level, where shock treatments were given. The girls came back subdued. One girl, especially, was full of spirit. She tried to run away and was given an electric shock treatment. When she came back, she was still spirited and full of beans but was returned to the lower level. I never saw her again.

I refused to stop meditating and refused medication. This was a serious mark against me. Nonetheless, I was moved to the highest level. This meant I could go home on weekends. Although I knew all was well, somehow, as far as my inevitable travel to India, it was obvious my present state of life was far from this and still very unstable. One day while visiting home, I connected with my school friend Lily from the East Village. She and her boyfriend were seeing a swami from India. They excitedly told me I must meet him. His name was Swami Satchidananda, and I immediately went to the large apartment where he was living and teaching yoga in a large old brownstone apartment complex on West End Avenue at Eighty-Fourth Street. I was very excited, picking up on my friends' genuine enthusiasm.

I was not disappointed. He was a beautiful human being and amazing yogi. I couldn't believe my eyes. He was physically striking, tall, thin, middle-aged, and very handsome with bright, soft eyes; long, grayish-black hair to his shoulders; and a full beard. He was dressed in a long, ochre-colored silk garment called a *dhoti*. The room in which he saw visitors was dimly lit by a few small lamps, but bright and warm with spiritual light. I waited my turn to go up to him and receive his blessings. I gave him a little vial of Lourdes water and told him it was sacred water from the holy place of pilgrimage. He asked, "Who are you?"

I answered, "I am Prudence."

He looked at me deeply and said, with the inflection of a question, "Prudence has come to visit me?"

"Yes, she has come," I responded, for I was under the spell of his divine yogic nature.

He took my hands, ever so gently, and looked deeply into my eyes. "Then, I am honored," he responded. I wanted to never leave. The spell was broken as I awkwardly pulled my hands back from his, not knowing what to do next. Seeing my shyness, he laughed. "Bring her back tomorrow."

His beautiful silence lingered with me. I felt enormous peace and intuitively knew instantly my stint at the mental hospital would be over soon, even if that seemed impossible. I became full of hope and joy, knowing I had spiritually connected with something tangible though unexplainable. I knew I would see more of Swami Satchidananda.

When I returned to the hospital, a doctor informed me it was arranged that I would attend a high school for the next four months and that I would reside at the hospital during the next four years of college. I would have loved to go on in school, but the thought of living in the hospital was unbearable. I was overwhelmingly depressed. When the doctor saw this, he said he had spoken prematurely and that due to my obvious depression, I was being moved back down to a lower level. There, a lovely lady named Anna, an artist, approached me. Her family had admitted her to the hospital due to alcoholism. Seeing my sadness, she embraced me, telling me I must draw deep from my inner strength. She said she knew I would be all right, that she could feel it.

Mia came to visit, and she decided I had to get out. We saw the hospital's head administrator, who looked over my records and decided there was no reason I should be kept there. I'll be grateful to Mia for the rest of my life. Of course, I made a beeline to Swami and went back every day from that time onward. I learned from him the yoga postures, called *asanas*, and anything else I could. I helped teach beginning yoga classes as I took more advanced classes from him. I went in the evenings to chanting and lectures he gave on the two authoritative texts, or *shastras*, of yoga, the *Bhagavad Gita* and the *Yoga Sutra*. Swamiji, as we affectionately called him, loved to make us laugh. He talked about its importance to health and how we all needed to laugh more.

One way he enticed us to laugh was to lie on the floor and put his feet behind his head, his arms coming out over the back of his legs at his knees and onto his chest. He looked very relaxed, resting his head on his feet. He then let some of the boys bat and swirl him around on the floor like a ball. I thought that was so funny, and I so badly needed to laugh! Sometimes, if he felt we sat too seriously around him, he suddenly broke into a fake forced laugh, which sent me doubling over. He told us of how, back in India, he sometimes deliberately tied his hair back in a woman's scarf so that when he was driving a scooter or open car, from behind he looked like a woman. He loved to turn his head when young men drove up close, shocking them with his full-bearded face.

Basking in the presence of Swamiji magnified my desire and need for my true teacher. I missed Maharishi, even though I had never met him. My life revolved around Swamiji. A group of us heard about an extremely effective special method, offered in Boston, of cleansing the body of toxins. I wanted to rid myself once and for all of the LSD residue still held in my psyche, so I took a twenty-nine-dollar shuttle plane ride to Boston with the small contingency from Swamiji's school.

We arrived at the doorstep of a huge four-story brick brownstone. A kind knobby older woman named Dr. Ann Wigmore, who held a PhD in religion from Harvard, met us at the door. She was the founder of the wheatgrass movement, and her four-story brownstone home was a treatment center. We followed her upstairs to the third floor, where several people between sixty and eighty years old sat eating a meal at a small round table in the kitchen nook. They all were very welcoming. Diagnosed with terminal cancer, each had come a distance to undergo the wheatgrass cleansing method of overcoming disease. This treatment was a last-ditch effort to survive, but I noticed their positive and hopeful attitudes.

Of the small contingency of students traveling from New York, one young woman named Katherine made enough of an impression to stick out in my mind. She was very pretty in a refined and classic way. She came from a large old wealthy New England family. I loved her stories about her extended family gatherings in huge mansions in old-fashioned grandeur. Another woman, Maria, also comes to mind. Maria also was very pretty, in an entirely different way. She was of Hispanic origins, from Central America. Her skin was tanned and her face strong. Her entire body was muscular and athletic. She underwent extreme treatment procedures.

Immediately upon our arrival, we were given eight-ounce glasses of warm freshly juiced wheatgrass. I managed to down it with relative ease, but over the next days this changed. In the cellar of this huge building, massive amounts of wheatgrass were growing in hundreds of long trays snuggled into tall dirt-filled racks. They were stacked ten to twenty trays high, on metal shelves with rolling wheels, and left to grow. An older man, a devotee of Dr.

Wigmore (maybe a boyfriend or hired hand) spent all day long, cutting fistfuls of grass to feed into the enormous metal processor. My prescription called for a large warm glass of lemon juice with honey first thing in the morning when rising. After bathing, dressing, and meditating, I downed a full glass of wheatgrass juice. I ate a breakfast of freshly ground cooked bulgur wheat berries and sprouted wheat toast with honey and melon, and then helped prepare lentil, mung beans, and alfalfa seeds for sprouting by placing them along moist paper towels and covering them with more wet towels.

Another glass of wheatgrass was downed at lunch and again late in the day. I was to build up to eight glasses of wheatgrass per day. I didn't make it. By the third day, I was vomiting blood. Dr. Wigmore advised that I continue my massive doses by receiving them through my rear end, by enema. After a few days, we were encouraged to fast. My friend Katherine, who also was receiving enemas, and I were rapidly growing weaker. Maria, with her strong constitution, was still thriving.

I got very sick and was forced to end my program. When he heard what I had been doing, Swamiji made it perfectly clear I should never have done this. He told me that a cow, an animal meant to eat grass, has two stomachs and spends all day chewing, regurgitating, and chewing again as a means of processing the grass. I got the message.

In Boston, a small group of people lived in a building with a Japanese spiritual master who taught Zen techniques and the macrobiotic diet. I met a girl from the group at the wheatgrass home, and we hit it off. We talked about mysterious methods of acupuncture and pressure-point massage. This group later formed Erewhon, one of the earliest macrobiotic and organic restaurants and organic food suppliers. I met all her friends and loved them. We ate macrobiotic meals—brown rice, lentils, bean sprouts, organic vegetables, and seaweed. They often ate fish, but I didn't.

Dr. Wigmore's house was like a youth hostel. People my age came from all over the country to stay there cheaply. It was full of people who had hitchhiked across the country without any particular destination in mind. At that time, several spiritual centers attracted like-minded people in the United States: Boulder, Colorado; Boston, Massachusetts; San Francisco (Haight-Ashbury), California; Los Angeles (Venice), California; and New York City (Village), New York.

One of the more interesting people I met was a nineteen-year-old boy named Tom, who had left his home in Oregon. I asked him why he left his family to come to the East Coast, where he didn't know anyone and had little money. He said that over a series of four months, he had vivid dreams that woke him and told him with some urgency that he needed to speed things up. He said when he was "awakened," he was still asleep but more conscious.

After this same dream recurred several times, Tom trained himself to be more lucid while dreaming. Finally, he was able to communicate in his dream and ask why he had to hurry. Two people, whose presence in the dream had been nebulous up to this point, answered his question: "Lauden is dying." They said the name in a foreign language he had never heard before, but in the dream he recognized it. They told him this name was a secret, never to be spoken to anyone. He had the strange feeling he already knew this.

Tom was very shaken after waking from this dream. During the conversation the two people treated him as if they knew him well, and he responded with an air of familiarity. The dreams were becoming more real, overshadowing his everyday world. The next dream woke him with greater urgency, warning him that little time was left. He was perplexed and paced all day, until he went back to sleep that night to find out what more he could do. This continued almost nightly.

It wasn't enough; Tom didn't know what to do. He thought, *If they would just tell me where to go and what to do, I would do it.* Finally, they said, "Lauden's death is imminent, so you must come immediately to Gloucester." Almost relieved, he packed his bags and left that morning. When he arrived in Massachusetts, he had no idea where to go or whom to see. His dreams had stopped short of those details, and he had no more dreams as he hitchhiked across the country.

As Tom sat on a park bench contemplating what he should do next, a familiar voice asked where he was staying. He looked up to see one of the two people from his dream. The person told Tom that he was a white warlock who had forgotten his heritage, that he was an heir to the one dying, Lauden, the head of the warlocks.

I asked Tom what a warlock does. He said at this point in time, one of his major roles was to help people avoid bad LSD trips and bring them back from the brink if they are lost. Tom said he fought the forces of evil. He pointed to his silent sidekick whom he said he had fought against the dark force to save. His sidekick Greg smiled as we spoke about him. Apparently it was a major battle Tom had barely won. Greg attributed his recovery from drugs, along with his sanity, to Tom's intervention.

Greg had been a drug dealer who apparently thought he was invincible. He was very charismatic and had a large following of young people. When he met Tom, he had argued and clashed with him. High on acid, he confronted Tom, who argued compellingly but, ultimately, there was a clash of wills. After hours of resistance, Greg succumbed to Tom's persuasion and was defeated. He now went with Tom and helped others get through bad trips, ultimately getting off drugs and turning their lives around.

I understood what they were talking about. I asked how Tom fought the evil, and he attributed it to willpower. Sometimes he used convincing words, he explained, but it was ultimately a mind game. In the case of his friend Greg, if I had been there observing, all I would mostly have seen was the two of them locking eyes, staring intently, silently unmoving for eight hours until Greg finally backed down.

One afternoon in a park along the Charles River, a lot of us were gathered to play music, eat, and talk. I got up to go to the water fountain, when a little blond-haired boy about five years old jumped in front me and chanted exactly like the Indian chanting I heard in the summer of 1966. He was very young and quick, and rather awkwardly darted away. Stunned, I followed him through the crowd. I wanted to ask where he learned the chant, but as I watched him play with his family, as I got closer, what I had heard as Indian chanting had clearly morphed into familiar children's nursery songs. I took this as a serious expression of my outsized need to be in India studying with Maharishi.

When Swamiji came to Boston, we were thrilled. One week we went with him to the countryside, where a student had offered her family's farm for use. We had a great time, and he went over the yoga postures with us as I continued to advance my practice. When we returned to Boston, my yoga continued under Swamiji's tutelage. His sublime yogic silence filled my daily life, settling over me with a timeless cosmic footprint. Everything moved serendipitously, as if predetermined or universally connected. Swamiji knew my attachment to TM and never interfered. I never thought to have him teach me to meditate. I knew that, for me, only Maharishi was the master in that arena.

Swamiji eventually taught his more advanced students to meditate when he felt they were ready for it. This was the traditional way yoga has been taught over the last centuries. First, the student finds an adept yogic master, a *guru*, then under his or her guidance does the physical postures, the asanas, learning and gaining more knowledge. When the teacher feels the student is ready to learn to meditate, the student is taught meditation.

Swamiji taught what I perceive as a more difficult method of meditation than TM (although he did not emphasize control), along with a more reclusive lifestyle. What I love about TM is that it is for everyone, regardless of whether they have the time, means, or will to change their way of living. It is a direct way to reach deep within and attain the ultimate goal of being whole and, therefore, the enlightened loving and wise humans we are meant to be.

nineteen

At Long Last

Except for a couple of very small courses held in Cambridge, Massachusetts, and New Haven, Connecticut, there was no place on the East Coast where TM was offered before 1968. No one had heard of it until the summer of 1967, when the Beatles spoke publicly about their TM practice. Suddenly pictures of Maharishi and the Beatles were everywhere. It seemed there was not a single newspaper or magazine that didn't have some kind of write-up about them.

Members of the press loved the exoticness of Maharishi with his white *dhoti*, long hair, full beard, and beads. It fit in with their vision of the young generation of hippies and their far-out psychedelic trappings. Meditation, swamis, and yoga suddenly filled the airwaves from TV and radio and pages of magazines and newspapers. As a result, I was hounded by paparazzi.

The combination of my being in the company of Swamiji and my sister's high-profile marriage to Frank Sinatra made me a natural target for media fodder. When Swamiji came a second time to visit Boston, the press got wind of it and photographers swarmed the area. I arranged a large lecture for Swamiji. With all the free publicity, he decided I should open a yoga school for him in Boston. So I did and ran a robust yoga center, teaching classes day and night to around six hundred students.

Yet, my desire to be near Maharishi increased. The more closely involved I was with Swamiji, the more I wanted my real master, Maharishi. I lived and breathed my prayer that I could study with him. In November, Jerry Jarvis, my initial teacher of TM, came to Boston. I implored him to ask that my request to go to India be reconsidered. He agreed to bring it up with Maharishi.

Mia also wanted to go to India with Maharishi, saying she needed to study with this saint, too. She and I are to this day deeply bonded spiritually, ever since our time in Marymount when we both wanted to be nuns. I had been telling her about TM and Maharishi, and gave her Jerry's number. She called him, and he connected her right away to Maharishi, who told her she could come in January and should meet him in Boston.

She called me and told me she was going to India with Maharishi, and it just about killed me. I waited anxiously to hear from Jerry, who finally phoned before Christmas to tell me Maharishi would interview me while in Boston and then make a decision as to whether I could go. The next four weeks of uncertainty were very difficult as my anticipation grew. Fortunately, I kept busy.

I had gained more responsibility for Swamiji's school, so he came to Boston more often and continued to give me more training and practices. Each wave of teaching bound me closer to him, even though in my heart all I could think of was being with Maharishi. I grew increasingly dependent on Swamiji. The influence of his peaceful presence was sublime. I was totally connected to him spiritually. I could feel his feelings. When near him, I melted. I would miss him deeply when I finally left to be with Maharishi.

January finally rolled in, and Maharishi was soon to arrive. Swamiji had just come to Boston, and we flew back to New York together. Jerry called Swamiji and asked that he meet with Maharishi while in New York. Somehow, Swamiji felt offended by Maharishi not having the courtesy to call him himself. Still, I was beside myself as the time drew near. I thought that if I were able to even just sit outside Madison Square Garden, where Maharishi was speaking, just being that close to the blissful presence of this great accomplished yogi would be amazing. The date finally arrived. Maharishi would be in Boston the next day, and I was to meet him in the early afternoon. I raced back to Boston via the commuter plane with which I was by then so familiar.

I got to Maharishi's hotel and walked into the room, where he sat surrounded by a few people. I was in disbelief of the magnitude and power of the silence he radiated. The peace emanating from him, from my estimate at the time, was three hundred times what I had encountered with Swamiji. It was devastating—I was in a state of shock. The experience was beyond my wildest imagination. I can only describe the power of the silence as like being at the center of the mother of all hurricanes. This was how vast the silence surrounding him was.

I fell at Maharishi's feet and wept from the core of my being, as if I was grieving for lifetimes of separation from this divine presence he was radiating. I was not so much meeting the human being—I was meeting my Self, the Self of all beings, God. I am not saying Maharishi was God, but he was an open channel, a vortex.

Maharishi dismissed everyone and then asked me question after question with acute precision and clarity. I told him about my life from the beginning, my spiritual experiences in great detail, my drug excursions, the hospital, and Swamiji and specific practices he taught me. With the precision of a surgeon, Maharishi cut to the core, peeling back hidden areas and probing deeply. I poured my heart out to him. After some time, he called Jerry back in and asked if he thought I should go to India. Jerry said yes. Maharishi looked back at me, put his arm strongly out in front with an open palm, made a fist, and said definitively, "You are mine."

It is said that in the presence of a great master of yoga, or guru, one doesn't need to meditate or transcend, because the yogic master is like a portal that allows blissful grace to flow freely into our world. This is what I experienced. The term "master," as in yogic master, can be best understood by comparison with the martial arts teacher as a master who exemplifies the art he teaches having mastered it. This is the same in yoga where the guru or master embodies the soul and teaching of yoga.

Maharishi told me to go to the hotel room next door and do my asanas. These yoga postures help ground the mind, and their stretching alleviates superficial stress collected in the body's muscles and nerves. The yoga room was filled with about thirty people, mostly teachers of Maharishi's meditation, some meditators, and a few members of the press. I went to the back of the room, along the sidewall, and began to do my asanas. Several people watched me curiously, but I continued my practice. After some time, we were all told Maharishi was leaving to speak at Harvard University.

Mia found me, and Maharishi called us to come with him to Sanders Hall. The theater, which seats a thousand, was packed. We sat just behind Maharishi on the stage, with about seven of his teachers. After the talk, we returned with him to the hotel. Mia's room was across the hallway from Maharishi's. I was delighted that mine was right next to his, so I could bask in encompassing peace that no hotel wall could block as I slept. I was in a daze, moving with my focus always on Maharishi. His presence mesmerized.

The next morning, Mia needed to shop for "Himalayan" clothes. I didn't want to go and leave his precious presence, but Maharishi said I should accompany her. He was right—she and I both needed warmer clothes because it would be very cold our first month in Rishikesh. We picked up my clothes at my place and then went to shop for her clothes. We were to return after lunch and join Maharishi on the plane back to New York and then on to India.

We took so long shopping that we missed the flight to New York. Maharishi had gone on! I could not believe it. As lunch came and went, I assured myself that no matter how long Mia took, everything would work out. Hadn't Maharishi himself told us to go shopping? When we arrived at the airport and the plane was clearly gone, I collapsed inside as my heart sunk. Mia was lucky that it was Maharishi who told me to go with her shopping; otherwise, my anger would have known no boundaries.

There was a lesson or test in this, but I was in no mood to accept it. Mia, optimistic as ever, was sure we would catch up with him in New York. But this was by no means certain, for we had to hope to catch a flight from Boston that would hook up with Maharishi's flight leaving New York. It was touch and go all the way. Mia had her personal secretary handle communication with Maharishi to explain we were coming and on what flight.

Our arriving flight did not make it on time before Maharishi's Air India flight was to leave, but due to Mia's and Maharishi's clout, the Air India flight delayed leaving for twenty-five minutes until we could board the plane. As we disembarked the Boston flight, an Air India executive shuttled us in the wintry cold across the tarmac among roaring engines to the awaiting Air India plane. I wrestled with uncertainty and fear all the way until I finally saw Maharishi's face once again.

Mia and I were about to share a most profound pilgrimage. We sat together on the plane. She had the window seat, and I had the aisle seat directly across from Maharishi. I could not believe we were really there and I was within a few feet of this indescribable powerhouse of silence. Everything was so far beyond my wildest imaginations. How long I had prayed and dreamed of being with this great masterful saint. Now I was next to him as he took me with him to India.

I reflected on how just one year ago to the day, I had looked upon the drawing, left on my pillow from "Lourdes." In immeasurable gratitude, I acknowledged that all this was through the blessing of Our Lady, the Divine Mother. She truly had answered my prayers. In awestricken reverence, I watched through the window next to Mia as our plane taxied and moved toward the runway for takeoff.

Mia moved to a seat in front, and I slept that night within a couple feet of my master. We flew through the night, stopping over in London. Maharishi carefully looked after our needs on the journey to India. After London, the next stop was Mumbai or, as it was called then, Bombay. We stayed in a hotel along the beach. Maharishi instructed Mia in TM, and I received further instruction from him. We were there a week before traveling to New Delhi, where we stayed at the Oberoi Hotel for another week. We had a lovely suite, and Maharishi visited us in the mornings. We saw him in the afternoons or evenings in a large beautiful home owned by some local Indians. I had the most delicious dessert I have ever tasted in that house. It was a lightly fried crepe covered with powdered sugar, ghee (refined butter), and lime juice.

We were told of several important issues to consider while in India—drink and use only boiled water, even for brushing teeth; eat only well-cooked food, no fresh tomatoes or thin-skinned fruits; in the cities, don't talk to anyone who offers to help you; beware of the monkeys, never looking them in the eyes; and always dress like the other women. But even with these warnings, nothing could have prepared Mia and me for our Delhi shopping experience. Maharishi had not wanted us to go shopping without a guide. But that day, a guide was delayed.

As we left our taxi, we were instantly greeted on all sides by vendors, peddlers, and beggars, all yelling at once, "Madam, madam! Here, here!" When we came out of the stores, rickshaw drivers pulled at our bags. "I'll take this, madam. Here, madam, come, come!"

Others shouted, "No, no! This way, madam." They pawed at us. "Where do you want to go, madam? I'll take you." They pushed one another. "With me, madam, with me." Exasperated, we were awash in a sea of madness. I unconsciously let a "no" slip from my lips as a beggar pulled at my shirt. This was a big mistake—ten more came to join.

I knew stories of India's street culture carrying people beyond their limits. I was experiencing it firsthand. Immersed in the crowd, I suddenly saw Maharishi's driver pull up quickly toward us. Maharishi's assistant jumped from inside the car and, almost miraculously, the sea of harassers parted as he moved his hands briskly out before him as if sweeping them away. With an authoritative voice, speaking firmly in Hindi, like a parent, he commanded the vendors to move away, "*Chalo, chalo,*" meaning, "Let's go." They scattered away from him like a pack of wild dogs caught stealing food. I was amazed. He apologized, shaking his head from side to side, "These people are a nuisance." Grateful, we were safe again, under Maharishi's purview.

The drive through the city back to the hotel seemed forever. I didn't care—it was all so exotic, the sights, smells, sounds. It is difficult to capture in words the richness of the teeming life where village, farm, and city mix together in an overpopulated stew.

I heard bells clanking from oxen's necks, cows mooing, crows cawing, and these sounds mingled with the incessant noise of cars, rickshaws, scooters, and the buzz of humans everywhere. I saw camels, elephants, water buffalo, monkeys, goats, chickens, cows, horses, burros, and many ox carts piled high with every imaginable kind of edible and inedible goods. The alleyways and streets were congested with vendors selling their wares off wooden carts laden with silver trays arranged neatly with powdered mounds of multicolored spices and leafy green vegetables, cabbage, cauliflower, tomatoes, potatoes, eggplant, chili peppers, bright orange gourds, okra, fresh gingerroot, sweet potatoes, exotic fruits such mangoes and mulberries, ground incense overflowing their silver bowls, stacked rolls of beautiful silks and cotton, along with richly colored scarves, bright shiny jewelry, columns of bangles, earrings, and cotton and silk purses. People also pushed wooden carts with huge mounds of colorful blankets, pots, and chairs. Beguiling colorfully dressed women in flowing saris were everywhere, as were men in white pajamas, white cotton pants from which our use of the word "pajama" comes.

Many shops were like big boxes stacked on top of one another, two or three stories high, in rows that lasted for miles. Vendors sat crouched on their feet in their boxes with barely any head room, fixing shoes, selling bangles and beads, pots and pans, and toiletries. Each block had a little temple, where a deity statue was protected, usually behind some sort of cage. Sometimes the deity was draped with colorful clothes and was always ensconced in the pungent smell of burning incense. Often, the temple priest chanted from behind the caged area, adding to the vibrancy and richness in the air.

What struck me most, though, was the sense of timelessness. Nothing was driven by time like in the West. People didn't even understand if we talked about having to be somewhere at a certain time. Back then hardly anybody in India operated by the clock. I felt as if I had taken a time machine into the Middle Ages. The culture was different, and time seemed to last forever in contrast to the modern Western world.

More than 80 percent of India's population still lived on farms. The pace of city life reflected the dominance of the agricultural influence, where life followed the poetic movement of the sun. This was my conclusion as I wrestled with the mystery of the relativity of time as I was experiencing it. A definite and undeniable silence also permeated the land, a phenomenon I had felt nowhere else.

Maharishi arranged for us to sightsee. We visited the iconic Red Fort, former residence of a string of emperors, in the center of Delhi. We traveled to Agra to see the Taj Mahal, truly one of the great wonders of the world. We went to Vrindavan, the birthplace of Lord Krishna, walking up the narrow winding pathways to the temple at the top of the hill. We passed little colorful shops and homes, which appeared to be buried in the hill. We arrived at the top in the evening, just as the temple doors opened to reveal the image of Krishna with his consort, Radha. The priest chanted in Sanskrit as camphor was lit and incense burned. The air was heavy with scent, and filled with the music of bells and chimes ringing throughout the town. People danced and sang, beat drums. It was extremely blissful.

Soon, it was time to move on to Rishikesh. Sixty-two course participants from all over the world had gathered in New Delhi. Maharishi arranged for several buses and cars to caravan up to the academy in Rishikesh, at the foothills of the Himalayas. Mia and I rode in a car with Maharishi.

I was still in a daze of disbelief. The whole time in India with Maharishi, I could not believe it was all really happening. The trip usually took well over four hours. We were leaving after lunch, but had to wait for everyone to organize their seating and luggage in the buses. It was a chaotic scene, between the shouting of vendors peddling wares, young beggars knocking at our windows, water boys running back and forth, and the bus drivers yelling in Hindi as they sorted people and their belongings into various vehicles. All the while, Maharishi directed people and the flow of activity.

Maharishi took charge of every detail of each person's needs during the trip and throughout the course. At one point, Mia turned to me amazed, expressing her concern that a saint would behave as Maharishi, managing every step of the way. Her image of a saint was someone like Saint Francis of Assisi, gentle and removed from the world. I asked her, "Just as there are different kinds of people, why can't there be different kinds of saints?"

Finally, we were ready to go. The roar from the great engines started up, and the buses slowly lined up behind our lead car, creating an atmosphere of excitement. I settled in, bathing in bliss and gazing out the window at the exoticism, prepared to enjoy the last leg of my journey into deep silence.

It took us more than six hours to reach Rishikesh, and we reached the foothills of the Himalayas just as dusk set in. As we neared our destination, darkness settled over the mountains and forest ahead, making the mystery of our journey all the more intense.

We piled out of our vehicles to walk over a fragile bridge across the Ganges, flowing loudly and rapidly below. The river was wide, perhaps three city blocks long. Along the walk, Indians trotted back and forth carrying luggage, shouting orders in Hindi, young boys laughing as they ran holding boxes and suitcases over their heads. Child beggars with their mothers pulled at our clothes.

The wind gusted up wisps of wet river spray on our faces and in our hair from the sacred Ganges racing below us. The bridge was lined with what appeared in the dark to be large full sacks of potatoes or grains. Later when I crossed the bridge in daylight, I saw that those shadowy shapes were not bags of edibles but rather beggars hideously deformed by leprosy.

The terrain became more lush and tangled. This area was called a forest reserve, but it was much more like a jungle. The air was warmer and sweeter from the dense green foliage. The surrounding environment was filled with foreign sounds, such as the eerie cacophonous cries of ubiquitous wild peacocks, the sharp intense calls of crows, and the loud chatter of bold monkeys. I realized that not only was I in India, far from home, but within India I was far away.

Cars waited to take us to the academy, situated along a cliff overlooking the Ganges. We bounced and bobbed as the car dipped and climbed over ruts and holes along the way. We were all very quiet, lost in thought. The foliage became even richer and denser, more jungle-like. I asked Maharishi how he had found this place. He replied that it had found him—the Indian government donated it.

Earlier in this journey, I basked in the peaceful silence around Maharishi. But now as we drew nearer the goal I anticipated for so many years, a quiet tension filled my body and I could not seem to recapture that earlier bliss. I suddenly felt uneasy and shy at the thought of finally settling in under Maharishi's supervision for the next three months or so.

After about a half hour, we reached the gates of the academy. A stone wall at the side of the entrance had the lettering *Jai Guru Dev*, ancient Sanskrit paying tribute to the tradition of yogic masters, embedded in smaller stones on its right side. Indians dressed in military attire let us through. They carried rifles over their shoulders, but I didn't pay much attention. I never knew exactly why we were guarded by the military, but they were all over this area of the Himalayas. Many ascribed it to the unrest between China and India.

Our car pulled up in front of *puri* No. 1, the first small building on our right. A line of six puris faced the wooded campus grounds, with at least six rooms per puri. All the buildings were primitive structures, made of cement and stone, painted white.

MIA AND PRUDENCE WITH
MAHARISHI ARRIVING IN INDIA
1968

twenty

Rishikesh Living

When I stepped from the car and put my foot on this hallowed ground, where for centuries, *Rishis*, or sages, had practiced meditation, I sank into deep gentle silence, instantly transported to a magical realm. In some ways, I was back in Lourdes with the sound of the rushing river outside the grotto. This was the sacred domain of the Hindu goddess Ganga: the holy Ganges River envisioned as an embodiment of the Divine Mother. I felt a sense of recognition, as if I had been there before. I felt in my soul that I never wanted to leave.

The people attending the course had traveled from all over the world. They were expecting to be trained as teachers of Transcendental Meditation by the yogi who developed the technique. My reasons for being in the course were far more personal.

The course consisted of immersing ourselves as much as possible in transcendence by gradually increasing our ability to meditate for more and more extended periods of time. Maharishi gave lectures explaining our deeper experiences, deciphering and clarifying the transcending process in greater detail, and laying out the scope of the larger yoga tradition of knowledge. At first, his lectures were held morning, afternoon, and evening. As our ability to stay longer in meditation increased, he gradually phased out lectures so there were none at all by late February. We were expected at that point to meditate at least eight hours a day, if not longer. Later he would change this formula of long meditations, finding it was not as advantageous to have us sit in meditation for extended periods of time. But I am getting ahead of myself.

When we arrived, someone asked Maharishi how he would make us teachers of TM. Maharishi responded by asking how we would spend most of our time. Meditating, we replied. He explained we would spend most of the next three months meditating because by steeping our nervous systems in deep transcendental silence, we were being trained to pick up infinity within us and deliver it to a student.

Maharishi led the way, showing us to our cozy rooms. We were each given separate rooms, warmly lit by candles that crackled and popped along the cement window ledges. The electricity was out. We learned this was the norm. It was very cold, and this gave Mia the opportunity to wear her new Himalayan hiking hat with its long side earflaps. I envied her.

The hard cement floors were barely masked by thin colorful rugs, which tended to ripple and bunch up under our feet. A richly colored Indian bedspread with complex patterns and designs covered the single bed in each room. The windows were large, with white wooden shutters that easily opened out into the jungle. We were given hot-water bottles to take to bed with us. When Mia mentioned one blanket might not provide enough warmth, Maharishi disappeared and returned a few minutes later with an armful of beautiful tan Kashmir wool blankets. He offered her to take two or even three. She apologized—she had not meant for him to bring more blankets.

Maharishi stayed late, making sure we were properly taken care of. We were brought hot milk with ghee and sugar and milk biscuits before bed. His voice faded into the distance for at least an hour, as he went from puri block to puri block making sure everyone was comfortable. I closed my wooden doors and climbed into my frosty bed, wearing every piece of clothing I had brought with me.

The next morning, still freezing, I did my morning meditation wrapped in blankets. I stayed cold for the next month. The dining room was situated near the cliff that overlooked the Ganges. We ate meals to the roar of the magnificent river below.

A sign warned, "Beware of Monkey Attack." There were stories of monkeys stealing entire plates of food. They were a great nuisance, racing freely through the campus, chattering and screeching above our heads. The crows were another menace, equally brazen, and also having the run of the place. Along with these were packs of scraggly stray dogs that had made the academy their home. They were a ratty crew of scavengers, who appeared to have dominion over the grounds.

The monkeys often amused themselves by tormenting the dogs, throwing bits of branches at them from the trees. They liked to torment humans also. Some mature English women lived at the far end of the campus. Every morning when we meditated, the monkeys gathered, cackling in the trees by the women's puri. One after another, they landed loudly on the roof, hitting it with their fists. Predictably, the women came out screaming and yelling, much to the monkeys' delight.

One morning as I was going to the lecture hall, an animated crowd of people was gathered. A tiger had wandered onto campus and was chasing a dog, so a military guard shot it. Another morning, a very loud and eerie wailing came from the nearby jungle. We later learned it was a water buffalo being eaten by a large python. Most memorable for me were the eerie whooping calls of peacocks, heard throughout the day into the evenings.

Because of the constant cold and lack of electricity, everyone walked around for the first month covered in head-to-toe heavy blankets. Most of the time, I was never quite sure who anyone was. Maharishi met us in the assembly hall in the late morning, after we performed several hours of meditation in our rooms. We meditated again after lunch until evening. This way we gradually increased our time in meditation. I was extremely excited at the prospect, diligently following Maharishi's advice. He reminded me to periodically do my asanas, which I did.

I was impressed that we all had easy access to Maharishi any time, day or night. He had a simple little house with a meeting room, bedroom, and small kitchen at the back. Below his bedroom was a small meditation room. A stairway along the side led to the flat roof, which provided extra space for him to meet people. The view from that roof was the best on the grounds. He also had a little garden between his house and the lecture hall. Some of us met him just before lectures to walk with him through the garden. Scattered about the garden were several little guest huts, made of thick entwined grasses. Scottish musician Donovan Leitch stayed in one of these huts when he came to visit Maharishi during this time.

Mia was not taking the course—she had only just learned to meditate—so Maharishi arranged for her to travel to points of interest in India. Time passed quickly for me, as I was preoccupied and engrossed in my meditation. One morning Maharishi called me into his room and told me, much to my dismay, that he had packed a lunch and a car was waiting to take me to Delhi to pick up my sister, who was returning from her Indian travels. I was very disappointed because I was just getting my routine down and building my time in meditation. He said I had to go. Reluctantly and annoyed with her, I climbed into the car to return to Delhi. All I could think was how lucky the others were to stay in this hallowed place with Maharishi.

I didn't want to miss anything, so I meditated in the car on the way to Delhi. Mia arrived in the evening, and we stayed at the Oberoi Hotel. Our room had two single beds, with a nightstand, lamp, and phone in between. Maharishi's latest instruction to course participants was that we should meditate as much as we could. I decided this meant I could meditate all night until I fell asleep. I was determined not to miss anything while not in Rishikesh. Late that night, at about three in the morning, the phone rang. Mia picked up and said it was for me. Suspiciously, I took the phone from her. It was Maharishi! He said, "Stop meditating. It's time to rest now."

The next morning, we were told the Beatles and their wives were flying into Delhi. Maharishi had arranged for several cars to greet them and bring them to the academy. Mia decided to go to the airport to meet them; I took a separate car straight back to the academy.

Back in Rishikesh, the academy was bustling with activity in preparation for the arrival of the Beatles and their wives. The young Indian boy workers milled around, carrying extra blankets, towels, bed tables, teapots, and water bottles, while their older counterparts swept the grounds, cleaned the rooms and bathrooms, and shouted orders to one another in Hindi.

Mia later described the mayhem at the Delhi airport, packed with a hungry mob of paparazzi fighting to snap photographs. She traveled back to the academy with John Lennon and George Harrison, and their wives Cynthia Powell Lennon and Pattie Boyd. Cynthia was called Cyn, pronounced "sin," for short. I wondered at the time how she could stand to be called "Sin." Mia said they were full of fun and good humor, that she laughed practically the whole way. Paul McCartney and Ringo Starr were to arrive later.

As I returned to the haven of my room, I was grateful for the familiar peace. I let the profound silence of meditation settle comfortably over me. I missed being away, even for a day. A knock came at my door. Maharishi had sent a messenger, saying he wanted to see me. When I arrived at his room, his brother monk, Satyanand, told me Maharishi was waiting for me on his roof. Maharishi sat cross-legged, on his deerskin, on a simple straw chair with his back to the Ganges. It was a beautiful afternoon. The sun was soft and warm, and a gentle breeze was blowing. I smelled the exquisite incense drifting from the rooms below. Maharishi greeted me with a warm smile and asked how my trip was. I told him how happy I was to be back.

He asked how I was feeling with the longer meditations. I told him I loved the longer meditations but felt my heart was still susceptible to flashbacks. He said my heart was filled with stones, which would be dissolved with more meditation. He reminded me my fears were not real but stresses, and that when I dissolved and healed those, the fears would no longer exist.

It was very difficult for me at that time to talk much about Mia. She had gained such fame, and it overshadowed my life. Everyone I met asked about her and Sinatra. As a result, the subject of Mia was a touchy one for me, and Maharishi was aware of this. As I blissfully enjoyed this moment with him, he pushed, asking, "Do you know your sister is a great person?"

Somewhat startled, I said, "No, I don't think she is a great person."

He laughed but continued. "Yes, she is a great person. Doesn't she want to do good?"

"Yes."

"Tell me all about what good she wants to do."

I attempted to respond, but I could not form the words in my mouth. On one hand, I was sitting before a very great sage, basking in the undeniable beauty of true peace and silence. On the other, something else vied equally for my attention. I could stay with this timeless moment I would treasure all my life, or I could give myself over to the demanding negativity, the stress.

Suspended for a moment, I watched myself from a place of detachment. Then before I knew it, I made my choice. "What kind of guru are you?" I yelled. "Why don't you just go to Hollywood, where you can meet lots of stars and ask them these questions yourself?"

I was horrified by my brazen response, and yet enjoyed the satisfaction of lashing out. He responded, "Now, go and rest."

I returned to my room, bewildered and torn by what I just did. As I sorted my thoughts, my awe for this great teacher spilled over. What an amazing lesson. I was truly learning firsthand about my stress. My resolve to use this precious time in deep meditation was resolute. I was determined to root out my stress, to be free to live.

After an hour or so, noise outside picked up feverishly as workers shouted out last-minute orders to one another. I heard cars pull up, and everything else was suddenly quiet. Then I heard the charming British voices of John and Cynthia and George and Pattie. Being shy, I did not want to come out as they unpacked the car, which was stuffed with suitcases. I heard Mia talking with them before they retired to their rooms, and the puri was once again silent. At dinnertime, I came out of my room just as John emerged from his. He boldly walked over to me, with the friendliest manner, and asked, "Are you Prudence?" I said yes, and he introduced himself. I immediately liked him.

I wasn't at all interested in meeting the Beatles because my experiences with famous people in Hollywood were often a letdown. I liked their music and didn't want to spoil that, but this encounter with John was a wonderful surprise. He was real. They all were. I was amazed. Maharishi asked if they wanted to eat separately from everyone to protect their privacy. They insisted on being treated like everyone else. John and George were the only two taking the course. Cynthia was exceptionally friendly and warm, as was Pattie. They did meditate but were not participating in the course. Paul arrived a little later with his fiancée, Jane Asher, and stayed a couple weeks. Ringo stayed just a few days—his wife had just had a baby.

With John and George there, I had course mates to associate with from my puri. Maharishi devised a safety system in which course mates, or "buddies," were put together to look after each other in case one got sick or depressed. The day after their arrival, we three met to discuss that day's lecture. I filled them in on what had been covered before they arrived, some of the material they had missed. The conversation shifted to more personal interests. George said he heard I was a yoga teacher. This fascinated him because he was a genuine yoga seeker. When Maharishi later asked which Beatle I preferred, I said I had most in common with George. Maharishi said that was because George was the most Indian.

My conversation with George and John drifted to questions of why we came to India to meditate. John said the reason he came was because of George. George told me he had his first mystical experience in San Francisco. He was the first to introduce the rest of the Beatles to hallucinogens. We talked about what was going on in the collective consciousness and how a major shift was taking place—our generation was breaking new ground. I asked George why he thought this was happening, and he said it was the heralding of a new time, that we were just the beginning of an even more powerful wave that would follow.

He said he didn't know why but that he needed to be a part of it. George believed this spiritual wave was very important and wanted to help. He talked about using his music to awaken people's consciousness. He was learning how to play sitar for this reason. He explained that Indian classical music, *Gandharva Veda*, was from divine origins and first cognized by ancient sages. Its *ragas*, or rhythms, mimic the natural cadence governing the twenty-four-hour cycles of time, divided into six four-hour periods. Ragas act like tuning forks, harmonizing and resetting everything back into the proper rhythms of nature.

I said that after meditating for three months in Rishikesh, we would never be the same. George agreed. John viewed what we were doing as more like magic. One evening, while walking from our puri to the lecture hall, John, who was wrapped like the rest of us in a blanket, peered out enthusiastically and asked if Maharishi would do mystical wizardry that night. Of course, I felt Maharishi was doing that all the time.

During our discussions, John listened intently, adding comments here and there. Almost like an outsider looking in, it was as if he envied our ability to believe, firmly, passionately, and with such conviction, in something so elusive. He admired George's way of bringing order to this unfathomable world. I related to George and benefited from his perspective through transference. This is why John calls me beautiful in the song—the beauty inside of me is compared to the beauty of nature: "The sun is up, the sky is blue, it's beautiful, and so are you, Dear Prudence…"

twenty one

Journeying Inward

The next time we met, both George and John had been doing longer meditations. George reported feeling the power of the enormous silence. He became aware that on a very subtle level past the senses, everything was more liquid. He could feel this during and right after his meditations. John was seeing all kinds of colors. They both found they could tap into their music in a way they couldn't ordinarily do.

While George and I had more in common in terms of how we viewed what was going on spiritually and in our meditations, as well as understanding why we came to Rishikesh and what this amazing course meant, John had the most acutely perceptive view of people and circumstances. Both were very funny, but John could peg people and things in a way few can. Of course, it was not always fun to be the brunt of his humor, because it was so accurate.

At one lecture, John sat in the front row. He turned his chair around and, instead of watching Maharishi talk, he observed our reactions. I didn't exactly know why he was doing that. During another quite long lecture, George stood up and politely told

Maharishi his talk was unbearably boring. Everyone laughed, Maharishi laughing hardest. One lovely thing George did was play music for people going through particularly rough moments.

As the course progressed, we were encouraged to not come out of our rooms at all. Little daily paper menus were put under our doors in the early morning to be filled out for the next day's food, which was delivered to our rooms. This program was not a requirement, but John and George participated as much as they could. Even with their continuous flow of business people and guests, they meditated at least eight hours a day for most of the course. Every day around lunchtime, I heard John compose and pluck out new music. He was intent and serious, spending most of this time alone. I almost heard him thinking as he plucked at one note after another. Sometimes George joined him. In the evenings, they jammed out in the patio area and invited others who played instruments to join them. It was sometimes very loud and spirited. They always seemed to have fun.

All of this activity in our puri, in contrast to the silence of the other puris, made me even more fanatical about gleaning everything I could from my meditation. I tried to get Maharishi to move me, but there were no free rooms so I had to stay put. I accepted this as my bad karma and focused all the more on my meditation. From the perspective of the people in my puri, my fanaticism was unhealthy. In some ways it was, but I felt it necessary.

It was about this time that my wire-frame eyeglasses finally broke for good. I had managed to patch them temporarily for weeks, but they always broke again. Paul managed to do an almost impossible job of piecing them together, but it did not last. I was forced to spend the rest of the course without glasses, relating to the world more from feeling than seeing. At night, I often had to be led around by friends.

We were expected to spend more time in meditation, and I remained in my room for longer periods. When I came out, I wanted silence. One evening, John and George jaunted happily into my room, playing "Sergeant Pepper's Lonely Hearts Club Band." Instead of cheering up, I felt worse, for I was terribly lonely in certain ways. Their coming into my room as *the* Lonely Hearts Club Band represented a cosmic irony. Another time, they burst into the room with their new song "Ob-La-Di, Ob-La-Da." I had been quiet all day, and although I loved it, it just felt unfitting.

Another interesting figure burst into my room one morning. I was sitting in meditation, and my spine hurt, the pain increasing. It felt like the energy rising in my spine was being blocked. I felt very uncomfortable. Suddenly, the two wooden cupboard-like doors to my room were forcibly opened with such momentum that they crashed against the walls. I looked up in surprise. A sadhu, an ascetic, wearing a thin jockstrap and dreadlocks rolled high on the top of his head, stood at the door. He grabbed me from behind, lifted me up onto my feet, and aggressively escorted me into the open courtyard outside.

Pushing me back down into a seated position on the ground, he hit the center of my spine with the palm of his hand. I exploded. The energy in my spine was released in such a way that I felt air pass through every pore in my body. I was bodiless, one with space, infinitely expanded. It was glorious. He pulled me back up, returned me to my room, pushed me back into my seated position, closed the doors, and left. When I tried to find out who he was, no one knew. Several of Maharishi's monks said they had seen him briefly when I described him to them. One said he had come down the Ganges on a log. That's all they knew.

I told Maharishi I was embarrassed and a little unsettled that sadhus, and even he, could know my feelings and thoughts. Maharishi responded that this was very good. I said I didn't understand. He said neither the sadhus, nor he, caused this phenomenon—I was the cause, and it was a sign of my growth. He explained that as an individual expands his mind, deepening feelings and consciousness, thoughts become more powerful and generate greater influence. As stress dissolves, and the deep purity and silent strength within the mind are dominant, the individual becomes an important influence for good in the world. But this gave me even less solace as I realized, uncomfortably, that I had not only disturbed the sadhu's meditation practice with my back pain but I had also interrupted Maharishi's sleep with my attempt at late-night meditation when in New Delhi with my sister.

All the while, I gained greater insight into the complexities of my stress. By praising my sister earlier, Maharishi awakened me to the potency and danger of my hidden stress created from recent years of living in the shadow of Mia's famed existence. Lacking confidence in myself had exacerbated the situation, increasing repressed feelings of anger and inadequacy. I had not realized how alive that stress was in me. I was very grateful to finally have to admit it to myself. Still, understanding and recognizing issues of stress was like trying to grasp quicksilver or mercury—it constantly slipped through my fingers.

One afternoon, I arrived deeply distraught at Maharishi's doorstep. My fear of having irreversibly lost my soul to the devil erupted once more. He sat outside talking to other students. I waited my turn but felt my dilemma was of paramount importance. I paced back and forth, off to the side. My mood turned from impatience to bordering on quiet hysteria. My face must have shown this. Maharishi finally said loudly, "Let me see what Prudence wants to tell me."

I rushed over and, speaking intensely, told him, "I am doomed. I lost my soul." As I was about to launch into further elaboration, I noticed he was trying not to laugh. Shocked, then embarrassed, I gained perspective as I suddenly woke from the grip of stress. Somewhat bewildered, I returned to my room to continue my practice.

As we ventured into more hours of solitude, I felt at times overwhelmed by the remaining two months ahead. Time seemed interminable, and I couldn't imagine how I would get through. On the other hand, I never forgot how much I wanted to be there. For almost two years, I cried out silently for this opportunity, my deepest desire. As I sat to meditate for longer periods, the draw from inside of me began to grow, pulling me quietly in. Moments were bathed in waves of bliss, drawing me further inward. I loved it. At the same time, a thought or feeling could flicker, igniting a sudden emotion or mood and then drift away. My deepening experience frightened me, as feelings from my LSD flashbacks rumbled restlessly beneath, like the shadows of sharks silently circling.

I thought about telling Maharishi, but then would be lured and lulled back into the ever-deepening layers and waves of experience. I couldn't stop. There was no turning back. My psyche craved the continued deepening, and I understood infinity. There was no end or beginning, and it didn't matter.

For moments, when I touched on those thoughts, I became frightened, but the feeling of infinite lightness and expansion freed me as it swirled around my darkest fears, gently loosening and massaging them, bringing light. I lived through earlier moments in my life when I could not cry or feel. Death shrouded my heart, cold and lifeless, sending a damp chill through my body only to be met by the gentle soft lull of silence, ever calling. I suffered strong physical pain in my heart and spine.

One afternoon, Maharishi called me into his private room, simple, not large. He had a single bed placed lengthwise along the wall to the left as you entered the room from the outside. He sat cross-legged on the middle of the bed, facing the center of the room. He had talked to me more about my stress and was following my progress very carefully. He had arranged for me to have massages. A woman from London on the course was a natural healer. The woman was there, sitting on the floor against the opposite wall. He asked me to sit between them, facing him. He told me to close my eyes and meditate, and continue meditating until he said to open my eyes.

I closed my eyes and meditated. After a few minutes, I felt my energy being sucked out through my back to where the woman sat. Then a huge wave of energy passed from Maharishi through me and back to her. The energy kept coming from him in tidal waves, bathing me. After some time, it felt like a delicate inner lining to my body was being ripped off from inside me—from inside my fingertips, head, toes, feet, legs, arms, torso, all over. Everywhere this thin layer was being peeled off and pulled out through my back. It happened very fast and with a huge rush of energy. At first, I felt a lovely coolness, and then suddenly, it burned intensely. I screamed out in pain and fell back on to the floor. I don't remember what happened after that. I'm not sure if I lost consciousness or just blocked the memory of the next moments.

By early March, I reached a point at which I could sit seemingly forever, floating deeper and deeper. I told Maharishi, and he said to remember to do my asanas before sitting for a stretch of meditation. I did as I was told, but this particular stretch pulled me into a state in which time was irrelevant, food unnecessary, and sleep nonexistent. I sat, unmoving in the full lotus position, suspended without body and beyond time for more than four days. I was always aware of a constant dark presence lurking in the deep waters of my fears, just outside my reach in the murky layers within my heart. Every so often I felt a rush of fear.

Late into the night as I crossed over into my fifth consecutive day of meditation, those dark shadows began to take life. I felt sheer darkness and horror. I was suddenly in my LSD hell, exactly as it had been years before. Overcome with utter terror, I yelled, "Get Maharishi! I need him—only he can help!" John ran to get him, and Maharishi came quickly. Only his remarkable presence could penetrate this. I saw him and felt his radiant goodness.

I cried out, "I am in hell again! It has come back! Please help me!" He stood by my side, and I took his hand, which radiated divinity, and buried my face in it crying. Maharishi stayed, silent, as I shivered and sobbed. His presence continued to shed light on the darkness engulfing me. He arranged for me to be moved to another puri. I walked closely by his side, feeling his healing energy as he escorted me to my new quarters.

twenty two

The End of the Beginning

Maharishi later said he was taken by surprise by the amount of stress he saw in my drug-addled generation. He encountered similar instances, although not as extreme, with other twenty- and thirty-something students who had used LSD and other synthetic drugs. After my experience, he instructed everyone to never meditate for more than twenty to thirty minutes at a time before doing some stretching asanas with simple yogic breathing. Stretching alleviates the stress accumulated in the body during deep spiritual healing, like taking a wet towel and wringing it out. The postures help settle the body and ground the mind. Only after taking time for asanas were we to return to more meditation.

This way the inward journey was comfortable and gentle, never overcome by extremely potent releases of stress. At the end of the course, he told me what I had gone through would never happen again and that the flashbacks would never return—the stones in my heart had been healed. This turned out to be true. I returned to Rishikesh two years later, able to enjoy a wonderful course for three months, never fraught with intense stress release.

During the remainder of the course, Maharishi often visited me or had me do asanas in a corner of the room where he was meeting people. If I stopped or my mind wandered, he tapped the table with his pencil or flower or whatever he had in his hand and said, "Continue, continue." Over three intense months, deep-seated emotional wounds were healed, and the dark intractable stones that restricted and crippled my heart were finally dissolved. Many times I cried for days, sometimes from sheer pain and other times in pure gratitude.

On the last day in Rishikesh, we were about to leave for the final two weeks of teacher training in Kashmir, John and George set to return to England. George sought me out in the lecture hall, where I was listening to Maharishi. I had not replaced my glasses yet, so I did not see George signaling me from the side of the hall. Someone told me he tried to get my attention and sent the message that he and John had written a song for me. They had written many songs during their stay, and I didn't think much more about it.

After Kashmir, we returned to New Delhi before I left India, under the care of Maharishi. He took me to Italy, and from there I went on alone to England with some friends and then on to the States. As I traveled back, I reflected on all I had been through and about what Maharishi meant to me, now that I was on my own again. I realized having a guru was the opposite of what I thought it would be. I had thought of the guru as directing the life of the student, but I was wrong. The guru's role is to show the student his or her potentiality. After that, it is up to the student, in this case me, to realize this potential by following through with the practices given me and to fully live my life in a balanced way.

I knew my personal time with Maharishi was over. Although I would see him many times over the years to follow, it would never be the same. I tried to understand this by remembering a story my mother told me. When she was hired for *Never Too Late* on Broadway, all through rehearsals, legendary theater director George Abbott rarely gave her cues or pointers, while he doled out many tips to her fellow cast members. She grew depressed and finally approached him, asking what more she could do. Surprisingly, he told her she didn't need his attention—her performance was good enough.

I realized on that flight home that it would never be the same because I no longer needed Maharishi. I wanted him, but I didn't need him. Although I knew this instinctively, I still didn't fully understand. I felt alone. I thought it seemed so hard to rely completely on an invisible guru. I didn't know what that meant or how I would do it. It then occurred to me that the finality I felt was the answer. It was over but not in the way I thought.

It was like the mother bird pushing its baby from the nest when it's ready to fly on its own. When I met my teacher, I met my Self. Maharishi showed me how to repair my wounds through deep meditation so I could discover my Self, by myself, in myself, not outside myself in someone else. This is what I truly wanted. I had to take flight, like the little bird—I had to live. As I bade Maharishi farewell, I said goodbye to the many dreams of my past, dreams that helped me believe and survive. I was poised to let go and embrace the unknown.

I returned to New York and stayed with my mother for a month before rejoining Maharishi, this time in Squaw Valley, California. One afternoon as I sat reading, my mother unexpectedly came around the corner into the room and put her head on my lap. She was crying, "I am so sorry. Will you ever forgive me? I had no idea, I had no idea." She had started TM, and for the first time understood its healing value. For so long, she had perceived my meditation practice as dysfunctional behavior. She finally realized its positive influence.

I first heard about the song "Dear Prudence" from a friend who heard it on the radio in August 1968. I had forgotten entirely about George saying they had written the song. I had anxiety about how they might have portrayed me. One by one, I listened as each of the other singles from India, recorded on a self-titled album, came out. Many were very unflattering, such as "The Continuing Story of Bungalow Bill" and "Sexy Sadie." I remembered John's ability to peg people and dreaded what he might say about me. I wished with all my heart he had never written the song.

My mother bought what became widely known as "The White Album" as soon as it was released in the fall of 1968. She introduced it to me in a most odd way. During a family gathering at her apartment, we were playing Killer, a whodunit game. The "killer" kills by winking at you, then you wait fifteen seconds before announcing you have been killed. My mother went around the room, showing the album while playing it on the record player. I listened to "Dear Prudence" with great apprehension. As each line finished, I wiped my brow with relief. As the song ended, I felt immense gratitude that it was not as I had feared. Just then, my mother came over to me, and leaning in, she gently said, "Isn't it beautiful?" I looked up at her, and she winked.

I never saw the Beatles again, but Mia kept in touch with them over the years. The Dakota, the New York City co-op John's family still lives in, is right next to what was my mother's apartment building. In the early '80s, just after John was shot, his son Sean came to my daughter's eighth birthday party. A mutual friend had invited him. A driver dropped off him and his governess. I never met his mother Yoko Ono.

Sometimes people ask why I never attempted to stay in touch with the Beatles. Having witnessed fame firsthand, I knew the lives of stars could be hectic and unpredictable. They had so many fans and friends vying for their company that I didn't want to impose on them, so I stayed away.

For years I had mixed feelings about listening to the song. There were many rumors and misunderstandings about why they wrote it, and I wanted to keep drama at a distance. In October 2001, I watched a television special that aired on TNT and WB, a tribute to John Lennon titled *Come Together: A Night for John Lennon's Words and Music.* "Dear Prudence" was one of the songs highlighted. As I listened, it occurred to me that of all their music, "Dear Prudence" embodies the spirit of India and, in particular, the 1968 course in Rishikesh. I felt honored and privileged.

George was right when he said a consciousness revolution was taking place, and it was beginning with the '60s generation. The Beatles, their music, and "Dear Prudence" embrace this spirit.

It's the spirit of a generation of people who could no longer seek outside themselves, for they knew the answers are found only within.

This revolution in consciousness continues with our children's generation and those to follow. The many yoga teachers spreading across the country and world, practicing greater awareness and teaching peace, are our children. They grew up knowing conceptually that happiness comes from within, and that by changing ourselves we change the world. But it will be their children, and their children's children, who transcend these foundational concepts to the reality of the Spirit, bringing this spiritual revolution to completion. We *are* changing the world and *must* continue making it more enlightened so all humans across this earth live side by side in peace.

This is the reason I am telling this story. After those months in India, in inexplicably profound silence, I am not the same, nor would I want to be. How could I? Spirituality exists whether you acknowledge it or not. It is powerful and, through God, anything is possible, *especially* peace on earth.

Many of us who came of age in the '60s continue our spiritual quests and know the joy of living peace. Before long, we will be gone—but others will carry our legacy. There is nothing more important any of us can do for ourselves and our world than for each to embark on our own unique spiritual journey within.

Epilogue

Overview of the Years since India, 1968

The school of hard knocks, for better or worse, seemed to work best for me. Nonetheless, after my first trip to India freed me of the shackles of my internalized stress, my appetite for life was insatiable, always outweighing any disappointment or setback. Quickly I would be back on my feet, ready again for the wonderments of life.

When I returned from India, I faced a unique experience—for me at least. Deep inside, I felt a confidence I had never felt before. At the same time, because I'd never achieved anything, my mind was in disbelief. When I next saw Maharishi, a month after I returned, he asked me about my plans. After I launched into a litany of possible options, he cut me short, saying it would be better for me to do anything, even if it is the wrong thing, than to do nothing. His response took me by surprise. Because I was afraid of doing the wrong thing, I suddenly realized I had been procrastinating. It was time—I finally had to jump in. Armed with the comforting thought of "even if it is the wrong thing," I hit a restart button.

My first job was in Cambridge, Massachusetts, in 1969, as a batcher in the massive computer lab at Harvard University. A batcher collected data cards from researchers, arranging them in a shoebox type of tray that was fed into the huge computer, which at that time filled an entire warehouse. At night, I attended basic classes at Boston University to prepare for college. I would later transition straight into university.

Once I got started, my ambition was limitless. There was no stopping me. Who knew? Maybe I could become a Harvard professor, computer whiz, successful book author, world traveler, and the list went on. Obviously, I needed to temper this new enthusiasm and energy driving my dreams. I lived with several others in a large apartment on Beacon Hill and rode my bike to work. It was a happy existence that lasted just shy of a year. In the summer of 1968, at Squaw Valley with Maharishi, I met my future husband, who was training to be a TM teacher. We married at the end of 1969, making it a particularly memorable year.

In India in 1968, Maharishi deemed me a teacher of children up to age sixteen. A final trip to India was necessary to complete my training. In early 1970, I left for another three and a half months with Maharishi. This time, my journey was entirely different from the first trip. I was not going for repair and salvation. Like most of my fellow students, I was going to become a full teacher of TM. I realized this time around, more than ever, how extremely fortunate I was to train under such a great yogic master. I once again vowed to spend every precious moment there in deep meditation. Over the years to come, I attended many courses and was fortunate to attend the last course Maharishi gave before he died in February 2008.

I was so much happier during this second course in India. I loved being healthy. The extended hours in meditation were even more profound and enjoyable because I appreciated and participated in their depth and serenity so much more. Maharishi's guidance from afar made me proud and aware of how much I had grown. I returned from India to the arms of my new husband and began a shared life with him that continues to this day. I was pregnant almost immediately with our first child, a son, followed by our daughter twenty months later. In 1987, we had another son.

Maharishi's philosophy was to embrace life with gusto, so I gave myself fully to motherhood and being a wife. My husband went to India in 1969 and also became a TM teacher. We have grown and made mistakes, while learning and embracing ever more deeply who we are alone, together, and as a family.

I knew then that this life would be my spiritual journey, that it would shape and mold me while ultimately liberating me. I knew that, along with my practices, if I gave myself fully, sincerely, and as honestly as I could to my every living moment, I had no worries. I could trust completely in life's powerful forces, which require nothing more or less than absolute surrender—letting go of everything and connecting with the one Soul, the great Womb of life.

After my second course in India, my husband and I lived in Canada, the District of Columbia, Florida, California, and New York City. The first several years of our marriage, we traveled as TM teachers with our two young children in tow. We believed in and loved what we were doing, teaching thousands of people of all ages to meditate.

In 1973, Maharishi formed a university in Santa Barbara, California. My husband was one of its founding faculty. After several years in Santa Barbara and Iowa, where the school eventually moved, we spent a couple more years teaching TM full time and then both returned to school in California. For my husband, it was graduate school, and for me, it would be just over a year at community college.

After that, I attended the University of California, Berkeley, for two years of undergraduate work in South and Southeast Asian Studies. I studied Hindi/Urdu, Sanskrit, Tamil, Arabic, and a little Swahili. I was in heaven, reading the original literature in its purest form. We lived in run-down student housing in Albany Village, but we loved every moment.

Toward the end of my studies, I took a work-study position in the university's Berkeley Art Museum and Pacific Film Archive.

The elite library and screening center, run by Tom Luddy, best known for cofounding the Telluride Film Festival, hosted great film legends and their works. I met many great film artists and legends, such as Werner Herzog, Akira Kurosawa, Fassbinder, Truffaut, Nicholas Ray, and Francis Coppola.

After years of growing up in a Hollywood family, it was in this setting that my perspective on the movie industry expanded. My vision of it as purely an entertainment business was transformed into an intense love for the art of film. It pushed me into a new period in my life. I entered film production, eventually co-producing my own film. I originated and developed the feature film *Widow's Peak*, which starred my sister Mia along with Joan Plowright and Natasha Richardson.

We moved to New York City in 1980 to be part of the independent film circuit. It was an exciting time, and I met many famous and interesting people. But ultimately, it was too fast a life for me. In summer 1986, my husband and I visited Maharishi in India to study *Ayurveda* and pulse diagnosis, as Maharishi trained doctors under the best *vaidyas* (Ayurvedic experts) of that time. I was fascinated by this ancient system of health care. In 1987, after the birth of our second son, we moved to Florida. This was a peaceful and happy time for me, and I taught TM full time.

In 1998, my mother died, and our family rallied together. The next year, I attended graduate school at UC Berkeley to study Sanskrit, fulfilling a lifelong dream. I spent eight long, wonderful years studying Sanskrit, traveling to India on and off, living with a Brahman family in India, and finally writing my dissertation. I received my PhD in 2007. I taught classes at Berkeley and Rutgers University. In 2008, I retired with my husband and family to Florida, where I write, study, and teach TM. All the while, my main focus is to enjoy a spiritual existence, embracing fullness in inner and outer life.

As I close this book, I would like to leave my readers with some final thoughts. Of all the good qualities my husband possesses, the most important for me is his wonderful sense of humor. He makes me laugh like no one else, even in moments of despair. Maharishi always asked if we were enjoying life. The spiritual journey cannot be complete without joy and laughter.

Maharishi wrote in his commentary on the *Bhagavad Gita* that humanity has misunderstood what all the great saints and religious figures throughout time have taught. We have studied these figures and tried to imitate their lives and works to be more like them. He calls this "putting the cart before the horse." Certainly doing good works selflessly is a wonderful practice, but what we have overlooked is the spiritual experience itself, going within. The reason these great figures in history were able to love unconditionally, do endless good works, see past the lesser deeds of others, and "turn the other cheek" is because of their inner state of spiritual consciousness. Their actions and behavior are by-products of that state.

We now know how to directly access this living state of wisdom within, thanks to the sagacity and foresight of the East's ancient seers, who realized its paramount importance. The practice of transcending in meditation, which they developed for mining this inner resource, is the best technology available to humanity if we ever hope to have a world living in peace.

Made in the USA
Charleston, SC
09 October 2015